'Pursuit of Happiness'

By Daisy Drews

Pursuit of Happiness

DaisyDrews

Print ISBN: 978-1-54397-565-9
eBook ISBN: 978-1-54397-566-6

© 2019. All rights reserved. No part of this publication may be reproduced, distributed, or transmitted in any form or by any means, including photocopying, recording, or other electronic or mechanical methods, without the prior written permission of the publisher, except in the case of brief quotations embodied in critical reviews and certain other noncommercial uses permitted by copyright law.

Dedication

To those who strive to make this world a better place.

Acknowledgements

Thank you to Deborah DeNicola for her editing of 'Pursuit of Happiness', Mike Taylor, and the support staff of Bookbaby for all of their assistance.

Cover Art by Randell Collins

Dear Reader,

'Pursuit of Happiness' deals with the extremely important changes in the time frame from the Glorious Revolution up to the American Revolution. The Wentworth, Bennet, and Palmer characters are fictional as are any characters with only one name. Their purpose is to highlight changes that are occurring. Other figures are all part of history and although their conversations, letters, or articles may not be literally exact, the ideas expressed within them are totally accurate. Let yourself pursue the unfolding of history as it occurs and appreciate the motivations and limitations of all those involved.

Chapter 1

The Shore of the Baltic Sea - 1689

On a rise in the meadow, a deer raised its head and listened intently for any sign of danger. Before him, the Neva River descended into the marshes that bordered the Baltic Sea. It fanned out into separate streams creating isolated islands. There was no sound to disrupt the stillness of this remote land. On one of the islands, a small, dilapidated hut was the only sign of human habitation. It had been thrown together to be used during the summer months by a Finnish fisherman. The sun sank in the west creating exquisite beauty as golden rays turned the clouds into God's artistic genius through nature. The deer lowered his head once more to graze on the soft spring grass.

Far, far to the east, over the densely packed forests and uninhabited plain, Moscow lay surrounding the Kremlin. Within its walls, Tsar Peter Romanov and his mother, Natalia, were now living. They had returned to Moscow after Peter's half-sister, Sophia, had made a final attempt to hold the reins of power. She had been defeated when the Patriarch and military had sided with Peter. Now that he was the Tsar, his mother felt it was time for Peter to marry and had arranged a union with Eudoxia Lopukhina. At first, Peter left the running of the government to his mother and her advisers and the foreign policy to Patrick Gordon while he indulged his love of sailing. He would disappear for weeks to Lake Pleshev. Although a shipyard had been constructed in Archangel on the White Sea, it was only usable two to three months each year. Peter yearned to have a navy and knew that he needed another outlet with constant access to the sea. The most likely way was through the Don River that flowed into the Sea of Azov, through an isthmus, and into the Black Sea. He and Gordon had attempted but failed to take the Turk's fortress on the Don guarding access to the Sea of Azov. Peter was now back in Moscow meeting with Gordon and his trusted friend, François Lefort.

"It's clear from our first failed attempt, we need ships on the water to isolate the fortress guarding the isthmus to prevent reinforcements from reaching them. Infantry and cavalry are useless unless we can destroy part of the wall. To do that, we need more powerful cannons."

"I agree, Peter, but where are we going to get the ships?" asked Lefort.

"We'll build them at Voronezh on the Don and then proceed down to the Sea of Azov. Mobilize the materials and men. There are many in the German Quarter who have the expertise. We must be ready to launch another assault this spring."

The second attempt to take the fortress saw the birth of the first Russian navy. Two battleships, 24 galleys, and many smaller vessels were sailing down the Don to surround the fortress guarding access to the isthmus into the Sea of Azov. Those in the fortress had called on their Tartar vassal state for naval reinforcement but when the Tartars arrived and evaluated their chance of success, they withdrew and the fortress surrendered. Russia now controlled the Sea of Azov.

* * *

At Versailles, Louis XIV was meeting with his ministers Louvois and Colbert de Croissy. The tension was acute as they knew their carefully laid plan for extending France's northern border into the Holy Roman Empire was now being challenged by Emperor Leopold I.

"*Ce n'est pas juste!*" I have a right to the lands we have taken. They are mine. Those fools should have accepted my proposal to make the Treaty of Ratisbon permanent! I clearly explained in my *Memoire de Raisons* the justification for our actions to fulfill promises made when I married my dear wife, Maria Theresa, and my sister-in-law, Elizabeth-Charlotte, has a right to the Palatinate."

There was a brief silence as none of Louis's ministers wished to challenge the king's assertion.

"Louvois, who will join forces with Leopold?" demanded the king.

"Well, I know that the southern German princes, Spain and Sweden met in Augsburg after they defeated the Turks besieging Vienna. Since the Turks are no longer an immediate threat, Leopold has also been negotiating with the north German princes and it seems he has promised to make Ernest Augustus of Hanover an Elector in return for the use of his soldiers. Leopold already has the support of Saxony and Bavaria. It's a formidable array, especially if the new King of England joins them as well."

Louis looked pensive and then resigned. He knew, as did they all, that there was no question of William adding his support to the opposition. "Very well. War it shall be! But we will keep William distracted. I thought his invasion would spark another civil war but I was wrong. The English fools support William. I'll send James, the legitimate king of England, back to Ireland. They have remained true to the faith and hopefully, the English people will see the wisdom of not interfering with the divine right of kings!"

Chapter 2

The Grand Alliance

William and Mary had ascended the English throne as Louis XIV sent French troops into the Rhineland. William had already resolved to convince the English Parliament to authorize support for Leopold I's Imperial Army against the French. However, when news arrived that James II, the deposed monarch, had landed in Ireland, William realized he would have to deal with that threat first.

At Whitehall, William and his wife and joint sovereign, Mary, were meeting with the Privy Council. "Gentlemen, we must recognize that Louis is our major enemy. It is he who has supported the pretentions of James and the uprising in Ireland. His money and manpower have enabled James to invade a land that is rightfully mine to control. This immediate threat must be dealt with but I urge you to convince Parliament to declare war on France. They are the real threat. I shall re-take Ireland once and for all, but after Churchill has re-organized our forces, we should have him use it to support the Netherlands and make it very clear that we support the Imperial forces aligned against France."

"I agree, Sire. Clearly France is trying to interfere in our affairs and I'm sure Parliament will agree to a declaration of war," said Godolphin.

"We will form a Grand Alliance and show Louis the wisdom of remaining within his traditional borders," said William.

Later that evening, William and his wife were discussing the meeting.

"I sensed during our meeting today that there was some consideration you wished to express but withheld. Was I wrong?" asked William.

"Frankly, I'm not sure," replied Mary.

"About what aspect of the decision?"

"Well," she paused, "about Churchill."

"You mean John? I thought he was very close to you and your sister Anne."

"I've known him all my life and he's a good person even if I despise his wife Sarah. Anne's too foolish to see how Sarah reeks of ambition, is so condescending and manipulative. Anne adores her. Sarah is all she ever wanted to be: beautiful, witty, confident," said Mary.

"But what of John?"

"I like him as a person but you must know that he was very attached to my father. When he was young, his family was having financial difficulties and John was made a page of James. He chose a military career and remember, James's brother, Charles, appointed James head of the Admiralty. But then came the bogus Popish Plot and ensuing Test Act. James refused to give up Roman Catholicism and had to resign. When he went into exile for a few years, he took John with him and upon his return kept him in his inner circle. When James succeeded Charles, he chose John to head up his military."

"But Admiral Russell told me it was John's defection on Hounslow Heath, followed by his officers, that convinced James to flee. That is why I made him the Earl of Marlborough and member of the Privy Council," said William

"I know and, as I said, John is a good person. But he was very fond and grateful to James. John is a Protestant and supports us, I have no reservation on that, but I think he feels guilty about his betrayal of James's trust."

"Well, when I first met him years ago when he and Sidney Godolphin came to The Hague during the Franco-Dutch War, I was impressed by his negotiating skills. One usually doesn't find such in a military officer. I think he was sincere in his efforts even if Charles II was not. However, I'll keep your confidences in mind."

* * *

By 1690, William had defeated the French and Irish forces at the Battle of the Boyne and James again fled to Paris. William sent Churchill to deal with the last two major areas that were still holding out: Cork and Kinsale. Churchill decisively defeated the Irish and returned to London but was disappointed that William showed little appreciation. Churchill was reassigned to Holland where he, and other English officers, resented command positions always being given to foreigners. Queen Mary's intense dislike of Sarah and rumors that John had contacted James, finally caused their dismissal from court. Although John's close associates Shrewsbury, Admiral Russell, and Godolphin protested, matters only got worse. On the testimony of a Robert Young who produced a letter that invited James II to return, Queen Mary had Churchill arrested and thrown in the Tower. When the letter was proven a forgery, he was released but, at this point, his military career appeared to be over.

Chapter 3

The American Colonies Express Their Discontent

In Philadelphia, Will Perkins had just received a letter from his brother who lived in Boston. While he, and his friend, Adam, were sharing a meal, he read and discussed the content of the letter. "It seems that King William has seen the wisdom of recalling Andros. Good riddance, I say. The so-called Dominion of New England was clearly only imposed to serve the king's interests, not ours."

"Does he mention the witchcraft trials?" asked Adam.

"Yes, it would seem that several young girls were afflicted by some sort of hysteria and claimed they had been possessed. Evidently, when pressed to account for their weird behavior, they were encouraged to name the demon that possessed them."

"That's disgusting. Witches are a figment of the imagination."

"Well, it seems they were believed and several of those they accused were hung, so, unlike you, there are still many who still do believe."

"I wonder why ministers don't denounce witchcraft as they denounce human sacrifice in other cultures. It's barbaric."

"Why should they? After all, neither of the Mathers, father nor son, dissuaded Governor Phips from bringing several of the so called witches to trial and seemed to support the use of spectral evidence."

"What do you mean, spectral evidence?" asked Adam with a puzzled look on his face.

"The possessed puts a name to the demon possessing them, eyewitness testimony even if the real person is miles away," explained Will.

"That's ridiculous!"

"Maybe so but most poor, illiterate people will believe anything if they feel anger, jealousy or fear toward the accused witch. Why are most witches female? Because they are usually without husbands and, thus, not subservient. Often they are outspoken and abrasive. Or, they may be widows who are now running the family business which other women and men resent or envy."

"But that doesn't explain why the Mathers would support such idiocy. After all, the father, Increase, is the President of Harvard College."

"I suspect there is a political motive. As leading Puritans in a very rigidly run Puritan theocracy, they not only resented Andros forcing them to allow the Anglican Church in Massachusetts Bay colony but, and this is only conjecture, now that he is gone, they see another threat to their power, the merchants. Boston is a thriving harbor and the people are becoming more secularized, thus the conflict."

"What about New York? Did he mention them? They, too, were made part of the New England Dominion along with New Jersey."

"No, he didn't but there you have the same divide, New York City and the original Dutch patroons with their estates centered around Albany."

* * *

When James II had ascended the throne, his Governor of the New England Confederation, Sir Edmund Andros, appointed Francis Nicholson as his Lt. Governor in New York. When Nicholson learned of the overthrow of James and the subsequent recall of Andros, he tried to keep the information to himself as he had sent most of his military garrison to help in Maine and New Hampshire against French and Indian attacks in that area. This made him reliant upon the American volunteer militias, which was not a comforting thought. He was wise to be wary.

"I tell you, now is the time to act," said Abraham de Peyster. "Nicholson lied. He doesn't care one jot about us. I say we follow our comrades in Boston and get rid of him."

"Who should we appoint?" asked Peyster's brother, Johannis.

"Let's leave it to the militia to decide," said Abraham.

"And what about Nicholson's Council?"

"We'll just have to see about them. If they're with us fine, if not, they can leave, too."

Official news of the rule of William and Mary arrived in June. Jacob Leisler was chosen to take command of the militia. When he and the militia took control of the fort in New York City with its military ordinance, Nicholson fled to England and the members on the Council received notice that they could retain their positions if they were not Catholic. However, Leisler made it clear that they had no real authority and, fearing for their safety, they fled to Albany. A committee of safety was created until official word came as to who would be in charge of New York. To speed this decision, Leisler sent his own representative to London to ascertain who would be appointed to replace Nicholson. Finally, word of the appointment and the arrival of a new governor, Colonel Henry Sloughter, from England ended the so-called Leisler Rebellion, which the crown saw as a treasonous act. Whitehall was displeased with the presumption of American authority and executed Leisler.

Chapter 4

The English Perspective

In England, south of the semi-rural town of Chelsea west of London, the manor of Thomas Wentworth was nestled among the beauty of nature. Extensive gardens, fields, and an orchard provided a variety of produce that would serve the city of London with sustenance. Flower gardens and boxes beneath the windows provided an array of color against the plaster walls and wooden beams typical of Tudor architecture. Inside the manor, Thomas sat at his desk reading the recently delivered *London Gazette* to which he subscribed. Having connections to the royal administration, it provided the most accurate information to keep one apprised of events within the kingdom and in distant lands.

"There you are! Come, it is time for dinner," said his wife, Anne. "Hurry. We don't want dinner to get cold."

Thomas smiled and rose from his chair to dutifully follow her into the dining room where their children were taking their seats. He took his seat at the head of the table, with his eldest, William, on his right and the two younger ones, Henry and Alice on his left. Briefly he looked at his wife and again smiled at his good fortune to have this cherished family.

"So, my dear, what is the latest news from the metropolis?" asked his wife.

"Well, it would seem that the Americans were even more overjoyed to have William and Mary as opposed to James than we were."

"Why was that, Father?" asked William.

"Well, it would seem that James, once he became king, appointed Edmund Andros to consolidate the northern half of the colonies into one Dominion with instructions to have greater uniformity, provide more revenue, and allow the Anglican Church to hold services; all of which incensed the colonists."

"Why just the northern half?" asked Henry.

"The original colonists in the southern half weren't, for the most part, religious dissenters."

"What's a dissenter?" asked Henry.

"Someone who doesn't accept the established religion," said his father.

"You mean like after Henry VIII established the Church of England?"

"Exactly. All were supposed to conform. But Puritans, Separatists, Quakers, people who did not conform to the new established order, left to find sanctuary in the new colonies. In the south, tracts of land were given to those who had leant the crown money and many of them were set up as joint stock companies. They had a plantation economy and sent raw materials; tobacco, sugar, cotton to England. The northern settlers, on the other hand, colonized by religious dissenters, were largely subsistence farmers. But, when New Amsterdam was taken from the Dutch, Charles gave it to his brother. James then renamed it New York and gave huge tracts of land to his friends. There were, as is inevitable, border disputes and, of course, tensions with the Native Americans that erupted in what they call King Philip's War. When it was over, the colonists, who frankly had no help from England, seemed to become disdainful of

English control. Once reputable merchants saw nothing wrong with avoiding our Navigation Acts through smuggling and began making some products, such as textiles, iron implements, and leather goods instead of importing them from our artisans, Andros was sent to tighten control."

"But doesn't that make sense," said Alice. "It seems foolish for them to grow cotton, send it here, and then buy the finished product back. It has to be more expensive than what they produce themselves."

"I agree with Alice. And to lump all the colonists together seems dangerous, especially if you're in Boston. I have friends at school whose relatives became Puritans and from what they tell me, Massachusetts is almost a theocracy under the control of the Mathers, Increase and his son Cotton," said William.

"Well, many of them agree with you. King William recalled Andros. So much for the Dominion of New England. His Lt. Governor in New York, which was part of the Dominion, was also confronted by a Jacob Leisler who had essentially established control there," his father replied.

Changing the topic, Anne asked, "Was there any mention of King Louis's actions in the Rhineland?"

"Yes, unfortunately. He thought he could force King Leopold and the German princes to accept all of his incursions into the Empire of the past several years but has been forced to retreat leaving havoc in his wake," said Thomas.

"Probably a wise move since Leopold is no longer distracted by the Turks. With Poland's help, they drove them back from Vienna and the last I heard, he's taken Buda in Hungary," said William.

"That's true and William may be our king now but he's a born and bred Dutchman who considers Louis as his number one enemy. On matters less disturbing, I also brought a new addition for our library. I stopped by the printers and he had just finished turning out John Locke's *Second Treatise on Government*. He told me that Locke had actually finished it a while ago but waited to publish it until after William and Mary came to the throne as it opposes Hobbes's absolutism with the contention that the people do have the right to rebel."

"Didn't Hobbes say that the people had only one choice, to choose the head of the dynasty?" asked William.

"Yes, but then it would be hereditary succession thereafter," replied Thomas.

"It seems foolish of him to assume that integrity is an inheritable quality," commented Anne.

"Locke would most definitely agree with you, my dear."

Chapter 5

Women Expand Their Traditional Role

The following week, Anne Wentworth and her friend, Mary Chudleigh, were on their way to visit a group of women who met regularly to discuss a variety of topics. As the carriage drove past the open fields bordered by orderly hedges, Mary was sharing with Anne her admiration for one of the participants.

"You will find the ladies we are going to visit are a very interesting group. Many of them have chosen to remain single and follow intellectual pursuits as opposed to the accepted role as obedient spouse. Mary Astell is one of the few who are not as well off but I believe Bishop Sancroft is giving her financial assistance until she can support herself. Mary is extremely intelligent and has been perfecting her writing skills. Her first book has just been published. Her rhetorical style in correspondence with a mutual friend of ours, John Norris, has been honed and her use of sarcasm and irony is bitingly sharp. Norris and Mary's uncle, Ralph Astell, were both part of a neo-Platonic group at Cambridge and he tells me he is very impressed with her reasoning and her challenges to some of his assertions."

"What is she writing about? Is it a novel or play?" asked Anne.

"Neither, it's an essay but, since classical education is restricted to men, she has developed a more conversational approach and is using a very personal style by addressing 'The Ladies' in a letter format."

"What is her intention?"

"Basically, she is a strong advocate of education for women as well as men. And although addressed to the ladies, she wishes to address men as well through the power of her argument. Her ultimate purpose is to establish a school for women which she refers to as a monastery, a retreat for women to develop their minds."

"But wouldn't men feel that was unnecessary and possibly dangerous to their position in the family, in society, in government?"

"Yes, that is why she argues that education will make women better wives. They won't waste the gentleman's money on frivolous pursuits."

Anne laughed. "How clever! I can't wait to read it."

The coach drew up to a cottage that was nestled among a variety of flower gardens basking in the warmth of the sun. Mary and Anne entered to be greeted with welcoming smiles by their hostess and the other ladies gathered in the salon. Introductions were made and Anne lost track of all their names but was soon engrossed as the conversation resumed.

"T'is a pity but wise of you to have your work published anonymously, Mary," said Elizabeth Elstob.

"Unfortunate, but necessary. It's interesting, if my rhetoric has intrinsic merit, ironically, most may assume it was written by a man. After all, remember the translation of the Frenchman, François de la Barre, *The Woman as Good as the Man*? He went much further than I have saying that women's minds are equal to men."

"He's a rare man to make such an assertion. Established tradition over centuries is difficult to challenge let along change, but I found your argument very persuasive. Hopefully, it will achieve your goal and we will have a female sanctuary of learning."

Later, when the ladies broke for refreshments, Mary Astell approached Mary and Anne. "Tell me, Mary," said Astell,"you're a friend of John Norris and I value your judgment. He has approached me on a matter upon which I have conflicted feeling. He wants to publish the correspondence he and I have had over the past several months. While I am flattered, I'm also hesitant as I was very open and honest in my communications. I feel that the reader will be very judgmental."

"The feeling of having something you consider private exposed to public scrutiny would make anyone uncomfortable but it is a very flattering request. And, his name and reputation will help with your ultimate goal of establishing a school for women. If it makes you feel more comfortable, you might ask him to keep your name anonymous as you did for your own work, which I'm sure he would do," said Chudleigh.

"That's true. Thank you, you have eased my mind."

As Mary and Anne rode back to the Chudleigh manor, Anne asked her friend how Astell had come up with the idea of conversations to impart her ideas.

"I believe she once told me it was from reading the works of Madeleine de Scudery. Fascinating woman. She and her brother, Georges, a playwright, lived together in Paris. She wrote novels, using her brother's name to publish her works. Her books included lengthy conversations of the figures involved, usually Persians, Greeks, or Romans. However, she was very clever with her words and descriptions and readers could easily identify modern leaders of society and were highly entertained. As her intrinsic merit was established, she also developed extrinsic merit and could begin to publish in her own name. She became very popular and was even made a member of the group that met at Hotel de Rambouillet and then opened her own salon. She is most definitely one of the first of her kind to do so."

"Amazing. This evening has given me much to reflect upon. Before my marriage, my parents never pressured me to consider one of the eligible men that frequented our house. When I met Thomas, it just felt like the most natural thing to spend the rest of my life with him. But, my experience is very rare. Most parents find suitors who seem to desire the dowry more than the woman or, if they are older and wealthy, they want a reliable housekeeper. I was fortunate, my parents did not force me against my will."

"That is true. The alternative options for women have always been very limited. However, there is great potential for women in the world of letters, even if they remain anonymous. Have you ever read Vasari's *Lives of the Artists*?

"Yes, indeed, but why do you reference it?"

"Because talent breaks down barriers. Yes, the first group of great Italian artists were considered mere artisans, nameless to the aristocracy, but, as their body of work grew and exhibited such incredible mastery, patrons became eager to sponsor them and the second generation of artists attained wealth and moved in the highest circles. Well, the world of writing is opening the same doors. More and more people are literate and printing presses now turn out all sorts of works. This will expand people's minds, their creativity, and stir emotional empathy. It may take time but it will happen."

Chapter 6

Peter's Grand Embassy – 1697

Nine years of war were drawing to a close on the continent. In Vienna, Leopold and Eugene of Savoy were discussing their options.

"We have retaken all of the territory Louis XIV was presumptuous enough to lay claim to. As the French retreated back to the western side of the Rhine, however, they destroyed all of the towns they had taken: Heidelberg, Mannheim, Oppenheim, Worms, Speyer. All were burned. And, although the British stemmed his ill-fated second attempt to invade England to place James on the throne, we might consider, as I am sure William has, putting out feelers to end the war. The devastating harvest in France and Louis's inability to import grain, has led to millions of deaths. Plus, I know his encouragement of French privateers has become a nuisance to English traders," said Eugene.

"That is true but first we must secure our border in northern Italy. That is where Austria is most vulnerable," said Leopold I.

When Victor Amadeus of Savoy decided that Leopold's aspirations in northern Italy were too extensive, he switched sides. Finally all parties agreed to end hostilities and the Treaty of Ryswick was signed in 1697. The balance of power had been restored.

As the Nine Years War ended in western Europe, back in Moscow, Peter and his friends came together in what was generally referred to as the Jolly Co., a group who drank together, shared stories, and drank into the night. On this particular evening, they were meeting in the home of Alexander Menshikov, when Peter made his announcement. "I have decided on a trip to western Europe. François, you, Golovin, and Voznitsyn will be my ambassadors. We must get the others in the Holy League to join us against the Turks. Also, I want to recruit more craftsmen with the expertise and experience that is lacking here in Russia."

"Will you be going with us?" asked Golovin.

"Yes, but I loathe court formalities and all that nonsense. I'll leave that to you," said Peter. "I want to learn, to see the advances there so I can apply them here. I shall go as plain Peter Mikhailov." Peter turned to address Patrick Gordon and Fyodor Romodanovsky, "I shall leave Russia in your competent hands."

And so the Russian envoy left Moscow and proceeded west. They received a rather cool welcome from the Swedes in Riga and continued their journey west. The first major stop was in Berlin. Frederick William, the Great Elector, had passed away and now his son, Frederick I, ruled Brandenburg-Prussia. Since one of Frederick's advisors had met the Tsar in Moscow and knew his real identity, he was invited to meet with Frederick's wife, Sophia Charlotte, as the Elector was not in residence.

When Peter was ushered into a salon, two ladies turned to greet him. He was struck speechless by his surroundings; the refinement and richness of the furnishings and the elegance of the ladies standing before him. He covered his face and muttered, "I don't know what to say."

The younger lady spoke, "Your Highness, we are charmed to have you pay us a visit. May I introduce my mother, Sophia, Electress of Hanover?" By this time, Peter had regained his composure and returned their salutations. Having seated themselves, the conversation resumed. Peter's gaze continued to wander and then focused on an object on a bureau between two large windows.

Noticing Peter's rapt gaze at a clock on one of the side tables, Sophia Charlotte said, "Ah, you are admiring Huygens incredible invention, the pendulum clock. Our dear friend Leibniz brought it to Hanover years ago. He had spent time in Paris studying informally under Huygens before he entered my father's service. Now he is the head of our Academy of Science here in Berlin. I hope that you will come visit us again. My dear husband will be sorry to have missed you. Let us proceed in to dinner."

* * *

When the Russian entourage arrived in the Netherlands, Ambassadors Golovin, Voznitsyn, and Lefort proceeded to the various foreign courts. Peter walked down to the public dockyard at Zaandam as Peter Mikhailov. On the quay, an older man, who had been carefully sanding the railing of a ship, glanced up. "As I live and breathe. Peter, is it really you?"

Peter smiled in recognition. "Gerrit, it's good to see you."

"I can't believe it. Last time I saw you in the Zemsky Sloboda you were what, 11, 12? Now look at you. How you've grown. You make the rest of us look like dwarfs." Peter laughed. He had gotten used to being taller than others.

"What are you doing here in Holland?"

"I need a job. I want to learn the shipbuilding business from the ground up."

"Well, I can certainly use you but," he paused, "considering your circumstance, won't people think it a bit odd?"

"Nonsense. My name is Peter Mikhailov and I am a simple sailor."

"Where are you staying?" Gerrit asked.

"Maybe you could help me there. Do you have room to put me up?"

"Well, my sister lives with me and could probably move in with her son. Sure, but I warn you, it will be very modest."

"Good. Just what I want."

Peter was soon engrossed in the craft of shipbuilding. Unfortunately, the local inhabitants started to wonder who the stranger was. His friends would come to visit and spoke a language they didn't understand and wore clothing that denoted a much more elevated station than the lowly seaman. And yet they spoke with deference to this Peter Mikhailov. Soon Peter's real identity became known and people flocked to see for themselves the Tsar of Russia. The Dutch government intervened and invited Peter to continue his self-education in the Dutch East Indies Co. dockyard and provided housing for the Tsar and his entourage. The public was excluded.

Over the months, Peter also traveled to other cities to observe and learn.

In Delft, he met Anthony Leeuwenhoek who was now famous in learned circles, had been made a member of the Royal Society, and continued to publish fascinating discoveries he found through his microscope.

"It's an honor, Sir," said Leeuwenhoek. "Welcome to my humble abode. Would you care to see my laboratory? They walked into another small room where Leeuwenhoek had set one of his microscopes. "Would you like to see for yourself?"

Peter peered through the lens and almost jumped back when something wiggled.

"You see, the naked eye can't see these little creatures but with this," he said tapping the microscope, "they are revealed. Over here

I'm working on something else, the circulation in the capillaries of an eel. I am convinced they are the key to completing William Harvey's theory on blood circulation."

When it was time to leave, Leeuwenhoek asked him if he was going to England.

"Yes, William has invited me."

"Well, you must visit the Royal Society. I've never left Delft but through correspondence feel that many of its members are my closest friends." He held out one of his microscopes to Peter. "A small token but I appreciate your interest. Enjoy the rest of your journey."

Peter set off for England and was warmly received by William. Queen Mary had died four years before so the two men could meet without the formality that Peter despised. One of his very first visits was to the Royal Society, where, upon hearing of his desire to stay near Deptford and its naval yard, John Evelyn offered his home, Sayes Court, as he now lived in London.

While in London, Peter visited the observatory, the armory, and the Mint. He traveled to Oxford and was impressed with the concentration of learning within Bodlian Library. Back in London, he attended a session of the House of Lords over which William III presided. Peter was surprised but appreciated that the members could speak their mind to the King. William also gave Peter a yacht designed by Peregrine Osborne, the Marquis of Carmarthen. Carmarthen and Peter became mates and, to counterbalance serious pursuits, Peter and his compatriots continued to enjoy the drinking binges of the Jolly Co.

Peter even visited a Quaker meeting-house in Deptford and was surprised the next day by a visit from two of the Quakers, Thomas Story and William Penn. Having traveled in Holland, Penn was conversant in Dutch as was Peter who had learned it as a boy from Andrew Vinius. They presented him with Robert Barkley's *Apology*, which set out the fundamental beliefs of the Quaker religion. Unfortunately, it was in Latin. Realizing that the Tsar could not read Latin, Penn offered to bring some of his own writings, which were in Dutch.

"As you saw in our silent service, it is a time for individual introspection and communication with God. That is why there is no minister."

"Why is everyone dressed so somberly and the men don't remove their hats, even for those of higher rank? Don't think I'm offended but everything in my church is so elaborate and ritualized."

"We believe in the equality of all. Those who prosper help those in difficulty. We believe in peace," said Penn.

"Is that why you don't wear swords?"

"Yes, we are opposed to violence."

"But if you are attacked, surely you defend yourselves?"

"No, we submit until others realize the error of their violent ways." Penn smiled. "Actually, it was the religious persecution that gave rise to the colony I formed in America. Essentially all are welcome, they elect their own leaders, make their own laws, and deal fairly with the North American inhabitants."

"It sounds ideal. However, where I come from it's still one clan against another. We need to change our ways. Thank you for sharing your vision."

While Peter was engaged in learning trades, his ideas were evolving and his mind played with how they could be implemented. His Ambassadors and representatives were busy recruiting artisans to come to Russia and help make Peter's dream a reality. Over the year that had passed since he had left Russia, Peter had also learned the art of watch making, gunnery, boot making and wood carving. The trip was expensive and the precious furs that they had brought to pay their way were rapidly diminishing. Fortunately, Lord Carmarthen was willing to pay a sizable sum for a tobacco concession in Russia. Peter then set off to visit the new king of Poland, Augustus II. Originally the Elector of Saxony, Augustus had seen the opportunity to rise to greater heights. When King John III Sobieski died, Augustus converted to Roman Catholicism, borrowed enough money to win election to the Polish throne, and had defeated the Tartars at the Battle of Podhajce, which made the Turks see the wisdom of signing the Treaty of Karlowitz. When he and Peter met, he was appreciative of the offer of financial backing if he agreed to further war with the Ottoman Empire but saw no reason to reignite a campaign against the Turks. However, Augustus shared with Peter another idea.

"I think it would be in both of our interests to form a coalition against Sweden. I know Frederick IV of Denmark would join us. Sweden's new king is Charles XII and he is young and ambitious."

Peter was reluctant to give up his desire to pursue access to the Black Sea and beyond but the thought of driving the Swedes out of the eastern Baltic was very appealing. And, it would achieve Peter's ultimate purpose, access to markets in western Europe. Augustus had signed a thirty-year truce with the Ottomans so Peter decided that as soon as he had done the same, he would join Poland and fight Sweden instead. Then Peter received news that the Streltsky had again revolted. The cause of the revolt stemmed from their loss of prestige following Sophia's attempt to take over the government in 1689. No longer were they the elite regiment that protected Moscow. Peter immediately left for Russia. By the time he and his entourage arrived in Moscow, the uprising by the Streltsky had been dealt with by Patrick Gordon. This time, punishment for all those involved would be excruciating. Thousands were tortured and hung. Those Streltsky who survived were exiled to Siberia.

Peter's trip abroad had exposed him to Russia's backwardness in all areas compared with western powers. Peter was determined to change that. Thus, the aristocracy was to imitate the dress, language, and etiquette of the French court. And yes, that included the shaving of beards! On more important matters, his ambassadors had hired hundreds of Dutch and German craftsmen and Peter set about improvements in his military and building a real Russian navy.

Chapter 7

War of Spanish Succession

In October of 1699, the long anticipated death of Charles II of Spain occurred. Charles had no direct heir. Before he died, he had written and sealed the name of his chosen successor: Philip, Duke of Anjou. The news was received throughout the royal courts of Europe with arrogant satisfaction in France: with dismay and anger in those countries that had joined the Grand Alliance against France and were still recovering from the Nine Years War. Before Charles II's death, William had attempted to find a peaceful solution to the danger they could all foresee when the Spanish throne fell vacant. He reflected on the upcoming meeting with his Privy Council, which again included John Churchill. After his wife's death and over the ensuing years, his relationship with the Churchills, both John and Sarah, had improved. Although he still had reservations, he knew that his remaining years were few and he also knew there was no one of military experience better able to protect the interests of England than John Churchill.

In Whitehall, the king and his councilors met. "Gentlemen, we are here to decide on a course of action. The situation is complicated. Since Louis XIV will not remove Philip from the French line of succession, the possibility of the two thrones at some future time being united is a threat to all of us," said William.

"It's ridiculous," said Sidney Godolphin. "Philip is a young man and Louis could influence policy in Spain without antagonizing the rest of us."

"Louis has been in absolute control and feels it is his divine right to dictate to the rest of us," said Shrewsbury.

"Be that as it may, we have a problem. Leopold I of Austria, the Holy Roman Emperor, feels that if Louis won't reject Philip's right to inherit, neither will he," said William.

"I don't understand. Why would he have the right?"

"Briefly, Louis married the Habsburg, Maria Theresa, and upon such marriage she renounced her claim to the throne of Spain. Leopold married her sister, named Margaret Theresa, and she renounced her claim to the Spanish throne. So, if Louis is now ignoring his wife's renunciation, Leopold feels he can ignore Margaret's renunciation. He knows his eldest son Joseph will follow him as ruler in the Holy Roman Empire and so he wants his second son, Charles, to be King of Spain."

"Well, for us, either one is as bad as the other because it means an incredible concentration of power in one king," said Godolphin.

"That is true but it seems that it has become more complicated," said William.

The others sat back, trying to deal with the problem they already faced. With questioning looks, they listened as William spoke. "My man in Bavaria has just returned and informed me that Max Emanuel intends to claim the Spanish throne for his son, Joseph Ferdinand. You may remember that Margaret Theresa and Leopold's daughter, Maria Antonia, married Max Emanuel and, although she, too, signed a waiver renouncing her right to the Spanish throne, it seems that the Council of State in Spain would be agreeable to having Joseph Ferdinand as their king."

William sat back and let them digest this new alternative.

"That might not be bad for us," said Shrewsbury. "It would prevent both Louis and Leo from having more power."

"It would also lessen Leopold's military strength as Bavaria has a very impressive standing army and Bavaria plus Saxony and Prussia are all striving for power in their own right which weakens Leopold's real control of the Empire," added Churchill.

"Therefore," said William, "I feel our best interests are served if we can find an amicable solution to this problem. I have decided to negotiate an agreement that we can all live with. To conclude such, I am sending the Earl of Partland to meet with the Duke of Tallard since France, at this time, poses the greatest threat. He will propose the following: Spain, the Spanish Netherlands, and Spain's American colonies to Joseph Ferdinand; Milan in northern Italy to Charles, and the southern Italian provinces of Naples, Sicily, etc. to Philip. That way, our interests are best protected."

In Paris, Louis XIV met with his ministers of foreign affairs and war to discuss William's proposal. Considering the strain on France's finances, they urged Louis to accept the English offer. Reluctantly, Louis agreed. But then, Joseph Ferdinand died before the First Partition Treaty as it was called, could be implemented. The Earl of Partland and the Duke of Tallard again met and a Second Partition Treaty was made. This one gave Leopold's son, Charles, Spain, the Spanish Netherlands, and American colonies, while Philip would get the Italian provinces with the exception of Milan and Lorraine, which would be incorporated into France. Unfortunately, Leopold was far more interested in protecting his southern boundary with Italy than having his son take over the waning power of Spain. But Louis rejected this and as a result, Louis sent Philip of Anjou into Spain with French ministers to help the young man establish control and he also sent a military force to occupy the Spanish Netherlands. War was inevitable. The futility of political diplomacy was exposed when it competed with the avarice of men.

With the outbreak of war, Max Emanuel of Bavaria, chose to side with France based upon the promise of being given the Spanish Netherlands as reward. The first confrontations occurred in the Spanish Netherlands as the Dutch had no intention of succumbing to this third attempt by Louis XIV to take over their country. They had held out before and they were determined to do so again. William III had made John Churchill the Ambassador Extraordinary at The Hague and Commander-in-Chief of all of the British forces.

Chapter 8

The Great Northern War

Redirecting his goal to the Baltic Sea, Peter sent Emilian Ukraintsev as Ambassador to the court in Constantinople to conclude a 30-year truce with the Sultan. He then set about building up Russia's military capacity. Members of the aristocracy were forced into military service and were required to provide some of their serfs for the rank and file. Armament was manufactured and uniforms made. As he prepared, Peter felt the loss of Patrick Gordon who had died that spring. The hundreds of artisans Peter had recruited on his trip to Europe were kept busy and he was forced to continue the practice of using foreigners for all but the very top military positions.

To solidify the informal understanding Peter and Augustus II had reached, Augustus sent Gen. George von Carlowitz to finalize an agreement. He was accompanied by Johann Patkul. Patkul was a native of Livonia who felt that Poland would be easier to deal with than Sweden as an overlord. The new king of Sweden also sent representatives to Moscow. At court, Peter met the formal delegation representing Charles XII to conduct the formality of renewing outstanding treaties of peace made in the past. Peter confirmed all such but would then go to Preobrazhenskoe to make plans with Carlowitz and Patkul for war against Sweden.

"So, Carlowitz, what is your proposal?"

"My Lord, our intention is to send Polish and Saxon troops into Riga to take Livonia and Estonia. You and your Russians will have free access to any territory north of Narva, which would include Ingria and Karelia. Most importantly, control of those provinces will fulfill your desire to have access to the Baltic and western trade. In addition, Denmark's King Frederick IV will be assisting us and this will force Charles XII to divert some of his forces."

Thus, Peter waited impatiently for confirmation of peace with the Turks. Meanwhile, Augustus, using Saxon troops from his Electorate, attacked Riga. It was an abysmal failure and Augustus's best general, Carlowitz, was killed. *Why wasn't Augustus there himself*, thought Peter. *Needless to say Charles XII will reinforce Riga and make it even more formidable to conquer.* He then heard that Frederick IV had been defeated at Tönning in Holstein. He chaffed at not hearing definitive news from his ambassador in Constantinople. Finally, it arrived and Peter sent Golovin with orders to take Narva.

By early October, the fresh water of the Baltic had begun to freeze. The custom had always been for armies to go to winter quarters while officers went to their estates to await spring. *No way*, thought Charles. Thus he told his assembled officers, "We set sail for Livonia!" It was a horrendous trip and many of the cavalry horses on board suffered and were crippled. When they finally reached the Livonian coast, the ships were immediately sent back for a second contingent of troops. With Carlowitz's death, Augustus had been forced to renew the siege himself but welcomed the icy winds of winter as an excuse to retreat once more. Peter, realizing he needed major reinforcements, had decided to return to Novgorad on the same assumption that Swedish forces would arrive in early spring. When he departed, Augustus had left Charles Eugene, Duc de Croy, in charge. Neither Peter nor Augustus imagined the danger that hovered on the southern outskirts of Narva. As the rain turned to sleet and then snow, Du Croy's lone sentry was petrified to see the Swedish army advancing on him amid the blinding snowflakes. Quickly the Swedes had made a breech in the walled fortification and the infantry stormed through. The Russian army's lack of experience, leadership, and training created a disaster. Hundreds were killed until surrender became inevitable. When Peter learned of the attack and humiliating defeat, he became petrified that Charles would march on Moscow. Fortunately for Peter, winter was a far crueler enemy, vanquishing the Swedes through hunger and disease.

Had Charles followed up on his victory at Narva by invading Russia, the Great Northern War might have ended differently. He chose, instead, to focus his efforts on Augustus's holdings in Saxony and Poland. In January of 1702, the Russian general, Sheremetev, used Swedish strategy against Gen. Schlippenbach whose anguished requests for reinforcements in Narva were ignored by Charles. Instead of going to winter quarters the following year, Sheremetev attacked in the dead of winter. It was a much needed military and morale boosting victory for the Russians. This was followed up with a second victory over Schlippenbach the following July with the establishment of Russian control over most of Livonia. Many of those civilians now without any defense were forced into Russian serfdom. Sheremetev himself acquired a Livonian man, Johann Gluck, a Lutheran pastor who volunteered to act as translator for the Russians and an orphan he had taken in when her parents died, Marta Skavronskaya.

* * *

Peter strode into the cottage in Archangel to meet with the generals Sheremetev and Apraxin whom he had summoned.

"Ever since my return from western Europe, my focus has been on building a navy and improved armament for the entire military. Andrew Vinius, my Inspector of Artillery, used the bells from our churches to make better and stronger cannon. He has been unrelenting in searching for new sources of iron. Now is the time to turn the tide against the Swedes. My information on a Swedish attack on Archangel was correct. However, the English and Dutch ships have brought news that Charles has abandoned the idea. Now is our chance to use their distraction in Poland to get rid of the remaining Swedish forces at Oneshka on the tip of Lake Lagoda and then follow the Neva River down to the sea. God gives time not to be wasted."

This is precisely what the Russians did and, with joy in his heart, Peter realized his dream of access to the Baltic Sea. This would become the heart of his kingdom. He was determined to build a new capital city on the immense swamp that spread out at the mouth of the Neva River. The Russian people were not pleased but there was no one who would dare deny him. The marshy wetlands were hardly the ideal location but protest was useless. The Russian aristocracy was ordered to send thousands of serfs to literally carry earth and stones from the drier regions down to fill in the swamp. It was backbreaking work but Peter, in his log cabin, was determined. Finally, the ground was solid enough to begin construction of the St. Peter and Paul fortress, a pentagon shaped bastion of stone. Again, these had to be brought in from distant lands. Tens of thousands of serfs lost any meaning to their lives and welcomed death as a friend. Just as the Great Wall in China rested on the remains of the dead, so would St. Petersburg.

On the recommendation of Andry Imailov, Peter hired an Italian architect, Domenico Trezzini. In addition to working on the Peter Paul Fortress, he was to build a navel fortress, Kronstadt, on an island in the Baltic close to the coast. Then, Peter left to rejoin his army. Here he discovered that his best friend, Alex Menshikov had now in his household the Livonian peasant girl, Marta Skavronskyaya. Peter had stopped by to see Alex but his eyes kept returning to Marta. His friend smiled. "Pretty, isn't she?" he mischievously asked.

"Yes, indeed," replied Peter

"Daria Arsenyeva, the young lady conversing with her, is my intended. My days of dallying are over. You might consider doing the same," suggested Alex.

"Your wife, Eudoxia, has been in a convent for some time now. Besides, she was your mother's choice, not yours."

Thus, Marta again switched households, converted to the Russian Orthodox Church and was rechristened Catherine. She remained a close friendship with both of the Menshikovs and became Peter's closest friend, lover, and then wife.

Chapter 9

Churchill's Triumphant Return

While the Great Northern War dragged on, war in Europe saw the Grand Alliance drive the French out of the Holy Roman Empire. Three friends were lifting their glasses to victory and happy to share their enthusiasm with all in the pub.

"We won! Frankly, I still can't believe it! Churchill was determined but I think even Prince Eugene was skeptical," said Reynolds.

"Who's Prince Eugene?" asked Liam.

"Eugene of Savoy. Actually, he's French but Louis never gave him command of a regiment so he offered his services to Leopold and fought against the Turks."

"I've heard of him. You say he was skeptical but he still followed Marlborough?" said Cory.

"Absolutely. He even gave Churchill one of his cavalry regiments to help defeat Tallard at Donauworth before they both forced the surrender of Blenheim. Eugene had kept Maxamillian Emanuel buttoned down in the village. The French were led to believe that Marlborough was going to Vienna. They never actually expected a major battle against their superior forces."

"What happened to Maxmillian Emanuel?"

"He fled to the Spanish Netherlands. It was incredible. Louis will have to think twice before he makes his next move. Let's raise another glass to Marlborough!"

In London, King William had died and Mary's sister, Anne, succeeded him. In the Queen's private chambers, Sarah Churchill brought Anne the news.

"Oh, what would I do without you and your dear husband? My sister, Mary, was always so unfair to John and so jealous of you. She never understood that John's loyalty to our father was personal, not political. I will make sure that he is well rewarded for his loyalty to me." Anne thought back over the years of childhood and conflict with Mary and her husband William. It had been Sarah who had orchestrated their escape from the watchful eye in Whitehall and secured Parliament's agreement to an annuity of 50,000 pounds. When Mary died and the Act of Settlement delineating the succession to the English throne passed in Parliament in 1701, Anne was allowed to take up residence in St. James Palace. A frown creased lines on her face when she thought about the line of succession. While she was pleased that it would exclude the illegitimate, Catholic son of Charles II, she was not pleased that it might fall to Sophia of Hanover, and then her son George. Although William had excluded Anne from government, his minister Sidney Godolphin was a close friend of both John and Sarah and kept them apprised of government attitudes and positions. When Anne assumed the throne in 1702, she had made John a Duke and Sarah became Mistress of the Robes, Groom of the Stole, Keeper of the Privy Purse and Ranger of Windsor Great Park; all positions of the highest order for a woman. Anne had even taken in one of Sarah's destitute relatives, Abigail Masham.

* * *

Queen Anne and her closest advisers, Godolphin, Harley, and Churchill, were meeting to discuss further consolidation of her rule. The Act of Settlement had excluded any of the descendants of the exiled James or the illegitimate son of Charles II. However, their descendants, living in exile in France, posed a potential threat.

"Welcome, gentlemen. As you know, I am very anxious to retain a close tie with Scotland and recent activities in the Scottish Parliament would suggest we move quickly. While we have had a shared sovereign, the Parliaments have acted independently of each other. It would seem that their recent Act of Security proves that they will not accept George, of the Hanoverian line, but will then choose their own ruler, which is unacceptable. Having such an independent sovereign nation on our northern border would be dangerous. Sidney, please share your most recent information as to these events."

"It would seem that the people of Edinburgh wish to stay independent.

And, it is most likely that they will choose a descendant of James or Charles. This, given France's enormous influence over any of these individuals, does not bode well for us. It was the French, you will remember, who supported James II's return in Ireland," said Godolphin. "And now we are again at war with France over who will control the Spanish throne."

"And to have Scotland as a hostile neighbor would certainly make us more militarily vulnerable to invasion. Plus, many of our finest officers and soldiers are Scots," added Churchill.

"That is true. Now, I have heard from my informants in Edinburgh, like Defoe, while many of the people are against union, there are certain individuals who are open to influencing the Scottish Parliament to sign a Pact of Union. Foremost of these would be James Douglas. He and others lost a fortune in the Darien Scheme."

"What was that?" asked Churchill.

"Back in 1698, a stock company was formed as an investment in the colonization of Panama, in Central America. It was a disaster.

Rich and poor lost their savings and Scotland has not recovered. If we make a generous contribution, I am certain that they will vote in favor of an Act of Union."

"And we will allow them to deal with all of our colonies freely. The dividends from such a union will well offset the costs."

"So, we are all agreed? Let's end this schism and become one."

In 1706, England signed the Act of Union and Scotland signed it as well in 1707. Thus, Great Britain was now complete.

Chapter 10

Dissension Within the Privy Council

Sidney Godolphin and Sarah Churchill sat on the settee in Godolphin's library discussing war on the continent. Outside, a heavy downpour made the fire in the hearth a welcome comfort but the expressions on their faces reflected their disquiet.

"As you know from John's letters, we are undermining Louis's control in the Spanish Netherlands and in Italy. After John's victory at Ramillies, most of the major cities have fallen. Even though the Duke of Savoy switched his support back to France, Prince Eugene delivered a resounding defeat to his forces in Turin. The new Habsburg Emperor is with us and agrees to keep fighting. However, I sense the Queen's ambivalence to our efforts and she seems especially prone to listening to Lord Harley," said Godolphin.

"You must remember, Sidney, Anne is a committed Tory. She has had one miscarriage after another and is often tired and sick. Her husband, Consort George, is no help; he's always in his cups. But I agree. Something is going on. I am often away from court tending to the building of Blenheim Palace and other real estate endeavors. Frankly, I get so sick of her lamentations and whining. But I agree. Something is going on. Lately, the Queen is often almost secretive. It's as though she no longer trusts me."

"Well, the Whigs are determined to persevere to prevent Philip of Anjou from keeping Spain. According to one of my spies, Louis did make an effort to have Philip step down but the boy is now a man and has no intention of doing so."

* * *

Churchill and the Grand Alliance would have one last victory at Bouchain. The French General, Villars, was deceived, outmaneuvered, and crushed, opening the road directly to Paris. But Godolphin and Sarah were correct that Anne had come under a different influence. Quiet, unassuming, always considerate Abigail Masham, Sarah's distant cousin, was also a cousin of Lord Harley. Harley convinced her to work on Anne's strong Tory sentiments to end the war and get rid of Godolphin and the Churchills. However, the following year, Harley came to be dismissed as a result of his own carelessness. One of his clerks, William Gregg, found confidential reports just lying on Harley's desk and sold them to the French. Anne was forced to dismiss him. Needless to say, Harley blamed Godolphin and had his revenge. Clergyman Henry Sacheverell, a zealot for the Church of England, gave an incendiary sermon in St. Paul's Cathedral. With dramatic fire in his eye, he gave his sermon *The Perils of False Brethren, in Church, and State*. The false brethren in the Church included all dissenting Christians from Quakers to Presbyterians, plus Jews, and Mahometans. He was especially vituperative against the hypocrisy of those who were secretly dissenters but claimed to be Anglicans to be able to sit in Parliament and enrich themselves. The false Brethren in the State were the Volpones. All those listening to this sermon knew that *Volpone* was the nickname Tories gave to Sidney Godolphin after he left their party and became a Whig. Although Parliament impeached Sacheverell, Queen Anne dismissed Godolphin. The Tories won a landslide in the House of Commons. The Grand Alliance army under Churchill would not pursue its advantage and march on Paris. A peace treaty was finally worked out. Louis would be forced to agree to separation of the Spanish and French thrones and accept England's Act of Settlement as binding. The Treaty of Utrecht was finally signed in 1713.

When Godolphin was dismissed by Queen Anne, the Churchill's fortunes fell as well. Harley and the Tories were back in control. However, the people knew who had fought for them and won the battle against the French. The Marlboroughs chose to leave England and the bitter memories of the Queen's lack of appreciation to visit allies on the continent. Here, the loss of favor at the English court was far less important than the admiration of the people: especially the Elector, George, in Hanover. Before she died, Anne repented her treatment of John Churchill and reinstated him. Thus, the Churchills returned to London on August 1, 1714 but Queen Anne had died that very morning.

Chapter 11

Triumph at Poltava

While the Grand Alliance was pursuing victory over France, Peter was determined to beat the Swedes. Their decisive confrontation would come at Poltava. The Swedes had spotted Russian scouts when Charles was inspecting his troops that had gathered for this major confrontation. A few shots were exchanged. When Charles returned to his camp, his aide waited for him to dismount. And then he saw that a musket had shattered the king's left foot.

"My Lord," he said just as Charles fainted and slid from his horse. The surgeon was urgently summoned. When he saw the remains of the foot in the smashed boot, he hesitated. Charles had regained consciousness. "Get on with it."

"I don't believe it," said Rehnskjold, head of the cavalry. "In all these years, not a scratch and now this."

In the ensuing days, Charles lay on a litter and devised strategy to defeat the Russian forces that had erected barricades outside of Poltava.

"Rehnskjold, you and your cavalry will take out the Russian cavalry and General Lewenhaupt and his infantry will march down the edge of this plain northwest of their army then, at this point here," he indicated the river Petrovka, "you will join forces and assume battle formation here that will pin the Russians between the river and this steep bluff. Tell Lewenhaupt and we will attack at first light."

Unfortunately for the Swedish soldiers, Charles designated Rehnskjold as overall commander. Jealousy, vanity, or just plain stupidity led to Rehnskjold not sharing Charles's overall strategy with Lewenhaupt. As the sky lightened to a pale grey, they attacked. But not having specific orders, Lewenhaupt devised his own strategy to meet the battle unfolding. The Swedes had also underestimated the number of Russian troops within their fortified redoubts and that they were now hardened experienced fighters. The attack was a disaster. The Swedes began to flee or surrender. Rehnskjold decided to retreat and two lines were formed to head away from Poltava. He was held immobilized by the sight before him. The Russian army, with Peter, had no intention of allowing them to retreat. Rehnskjold whirled around and finally saw Lewenhaupt with what was left of his infantry. "Lewenhaupt – attack at once!" he cried.

Lewenhaupt did as he was ordered and many of his men fell from the cannonades of fire from the opposing forces. Amazingly, his contingent broke through and he looked back expecting to see Rehnskjold's cavalry following up but it didn't appear. There was an ever-widening gap between Swedish infantry and cavalry forces. Peter, joined by his reserves, attacked again. The Swedes continued to die where they stood. When Rehnskjold was captured, Charles tried to rally his men but then fire killed or scattered those who bore his litter. A Swedish officer, seeing Charles's predicament, was able to lift him onto a horse and get him to relative safety at the rear. Lewenhaupt collected those who were left and withdrew leaving the Cossacks to discourage Russian pursuit.

Charles knew that when Peter realized how devastated the Swedish army really was, he would pursue. Thus, at the Dnieper River, Charles, lying in a wagon, decided to cross the river and seek sanctuary with Peter's foe, the Ottoman Turks. Lewenhaupt remained behind and began to march north as a diversion but was met by Menshikov's dragoons. Lewenhaupt knew it was over and promptly surrendered.

Meanwhile Charles had bribed the Pasha of Ochakov to provide boats to cross the Bug River into Ottoman Territory. Charles made it to the far shore but the once invincible Swedish army was sadly diminished.

The aftermath of victory over the Swedes at Poltava was stunning. Russia was now seen as a major player in the new balance of power. Peter's son by Eudoxia, Alexis, had married Charlotte, daughter of the King of Poland. Many of the smaller principalities within the Holy Roman Empire saw the opportunity to gain an ally through the age-old practice of royal marriage. One such was Duke Karl Leopold of Mecklenburg, who sent a betrothal ring to St. Petersburg with a proposal of marriage to _____ . The choice of bride was left to Peter! Thus, one of the daughters of Peter's half-brother, Ivan, married Karl and another daughter, Anne, was married off to the Duke of Courland. The Great Northern War was over and the war that France had instigated was ending through negotiation. A high price had been paid by many of those who were maimed or died in these horrendous conflicts.

* * *

Although England had not seen battle directly, all were relieved to have the war concluded. In Chelsea, in the garden of the manor, Alice and William Bennet, were enjoying afternoon tea while their young son and daughter played on the grass. Alice, formerly Alice Wentworth, had found a mate in William Bennet who treated her like an equal, respected her mind, and appreciated her efforts to help women succeed.

"Men are such imbeciles!" declared Alice.

William laughed. "Alas, so true, but what has elicited this current stricture?" he asked good-naturedly.

"Have you read the terms of the Treaty of Utrecht? The French have agreed to never join the thrones of France and Spain should it fall to Philip, Duke of Anjou, who is now the King of Spain. This is what the alliance had originally asked for. But do you realize the millions who have died, millions who are still suffering? For what? To satisfy one man's ego! War should be abolished!"

"Actually, dear wife, I agree. That is why I have chosen diplomacy over a military career. The few who are determined to augment their power, prestige, and wealth must be stopped. When leaders act for the people they are supposed to serve, diplomacy works. Unfortunately, there are too many rulers such as Louis XIV whose ego can never be satisfied. However, we, here in England, are at least headed in the right direction of a sharing and limiting of royal power."

"The sharing seems very limited to me," said Alice sarcastically. "Other than the male aristocrats and gentry, of course."

William couldn't suppress his smile. But, before she took umbrage, he asked if she had enjoyed Astell's latest work, *Proposal to the Ladies*. "Of course," she replied. "I love working with her at the Soldiers Hospital, educating the female children. Although she hasn't been successful in getting funding for a monastery of learning for women, she is doing what she loves."

"Well, may I suggest that the next time I go to the metropolis, you may wish to accompany me. Addison, remember, the fellow who started *Spectator* with Steele, has written a new play, *Cato, a Tragedy*, which all say, is fantastic."

"What it is about?" asked Alice.

"Cato was the one who tried to keep Caesar from destroying the Republic. He stood for the principles of virtue and liberty. An inspiring concept which I wish more rulers would consider."

William then shared his views on their new king, George I. "It should be interesting. Even those who strongly support the Stuarts have not supported the latest attempt to reinstate James Charles Stuart, the Catholic pretender to the throne. The Tories are seen as Catholic-leaning and I suspect Lord Harley and Bolingbroke will soon again be out of power. The stakes are different. George is a German and loves his country, Hanover. He has had more than enough time since the Act of Settlement in 1701 to learn English but has not bothered to do so. Anne refused to allow his mother to set foot in England and I'm sure she exulted in Sophia's death a month before her own. George's lack of concern and interest in English affairs will create a vacuum and I suspect the Whigs will be rubbing their hands in glee."

"The Whigs are the ones who pushed us into the last war. Does that mean we'll have another?"

"No, because the situation on the continent is different. Louis will soon be gone and the regent for little Louis XV has no desire to assert himself. In Austria, Joseph's reign was short and now they have Charles who has no more reason to assert his right to the Spanish throne. Sweden's power is fading fast and Russia is rising but they have a great deal to do and Peter knows it. Prussia now has a king and superb military but who knows how the future will go."

"I thought Brandenburg-Prussia was an electorate," said Alice.

"It was but Leopold I agreed to allowing Frederick to assume the title of King of Prussia in return for his support in the war against Louis XIV."

Chapter 12

A Comparison of Cultures

When Louis XIV died, the heir to the throne, Louis XV, his great-grandson, was five years old. Management of France during his regency fell to Philippe, Duc d'Orléans. Philippe preferred to remain in Paris at his residence, the Palais-Royal, with young Louis at Tuilleries Palace. The cafés thrived and the aristocracy enjoyed their soirées, the theatre, and the arts. The terrible harvests of the 1690s and that of 1709 receded and slowly the peasants recuperated. The rigidity of class structure and the Roman Catholic Church's resurgence continued.

At the Salon of Mme. Du Deffand, Nicolas Fréret was conversing with his friend, Arcadio Huang, who had been hired by Louis XIV as his interpreter and librarian, cataloging Chinese works for the royal library as well as developing a Chinese-French lexicon. Also participating in the salon was Charles Louis de Secondat, Baron de Montesquieu. Unlike many of his peers, Montesquieu felt that the French privileged aristocracy and the pervasive Roman Catholic Church needed reform. He was intrigued by the young Chinese man and they arranged to meet privately.

"So, Arcadio, how did you come to be here, in Paris?"

"Ah, it was not my original intention. Back home, in Hinghua, I studied with the Jesuit missionaries. They have done incredible work in China, expanding our knowledge of astronomy and mathematics as well as demonstrating a seriousness of purpose and dedication to their work, which I found admirable. I was amenable to following in my benefactors' footsteps and carrying on their work. However, when I first arrived with the Bishop of Rosalie in England and then traveled to Rome I had a change of heart. In Rome, I had additional training and was to be presented to the Pope but everything here is different. It is difficult to explain but the Church here has neither an intellectual endeavor nor real commitment to help the vast multitude as the Fathers did in China. I came to feel that my great Emperor, Kang'Xi, had greater compassion and care for his people than the cardinals and bishops I met in Rome. And, I will admit, exposure to your secular pursuits in science, philosophy, actually, everything, was more intriguing. While the Chinese do not get to choose their emperor, Kang'Xi seems much more sensitive to all their needs. Your former king seemed much more intent on gratifying his complete control in power over the people rather than gratifying their needs. Nevertheless, I do appreciate the opportunity to work at court," said Arcadio.

"You say they don't get to choose their emperor. How is it determined? Haven't there been several dynasties where power has changed hands?"

"Yes, that is true. If the nobles feel that an Emperor has lost the Mandate of Heaven and all are enduring great suffering, they will follow a new ruler. Thus, when the Ming leadership deteriorated, the leaders, especially Han soldiers, welcomed the Manchurian Qing dynasty. The real difference between your country and mine is that we don't have primogeniture. The eldest son does not automatically become the next ruler. The Emperor designates which of his sons will succeed him."

"Interesting. Have you had any recent news from your homeland?"

"Yes, they too have just finished battling but there it seems more justified. The Tibetans called upon Kang'Xi because the Dzungars had attacked them. Most Tibetans are Buddhists and follow the Dalai Lama. It is a very passive culture. They appreciated the Emperor's help and he is content to have the Dalai Lamas continue to oversee internal affairs."

"As President of the Bordeaux Parliament, I try to study, to compare and contrast the laws of various governments to improve our system. Well, I must be off. I promised to accompany you to the Louvre. Shall we meet there before Mme. du Deffand's salon next week?"

"I look forward to it."

As he walked home, Montesquieu reflected on the differences between the two cultures. He was impressed by Kang'Xi's rule of fairness, frugality, and morality. It made him reflect on how frivolous and wasteful were those who pandered to the king in order to gain material rewards. He also reflected on the suffering so many in France had felt from famine caused by poor harvests and war. He felt anger at the power of the Church that did little to improve the morality of the people but seemed just as venal as the aristocrats, rigid in its intolerance of any competition to its privileged status.

* * *

Clouds rolled across the sky above the square in front of the Louvre, once the formal residence of the king. When Louis had moved the court permanently to Versailles, he had left many of the royal works of art and designated that the Louvre become an art museum. As Arcadio Huang and Montesquieu entered the building and leisurely strolled through the wide ornate halls, Montesquieu asked, "Tell me, what is the art like in China?"

"It is far less dramatic. Here artists have used chiaroscuro to heighten the tension of a scene, focusing light on the face or action with a blackened background. That is impossible for our artists."

"Really? Why? Why are you laughing?"

"Well," replied Arcadio, "before I left I met a young Jesuit, Giuseppe Castiglione, who Kang'Xi hired as an artist. I remember his frustration as he adapted to our way. You see we do not use oils on canvas. Rather they are like watercolors on silk. If you make a mistake, you can't paint over it. Dark patches look like accidental blots on the work. Poor fellow, he was so frustrated, however, he was good and has adapted. Actually, the most beautiful piece of art I have ever seen was done by some unknown artist just using beige silk thread. The trees, the flowing river, and the swaying reeds, different stitching and the light reflecting made it come alive. You could feel the breeze and hear the gentle gurgle of water,"

As they strolled down the long gallery Montesquieu said, "Artwork here broke the rigidity of the social hierarchy, first in Italy, then with the Dutch masters and now throughout Europe. The Protestant reformation helped expand literacy everywhere and now the Republic of Letters facilitates the growth of knowledge and the diffusion of ideas. When you were at Versailles, did you see the work of Leonardo da Vinci? I believe he called it *Mona Lisa* which he painted for her husband, Francesco del Giocondo, but elected to keep for himself."

"Ah, yes, Louis kept it in his bedroom. I caught a glimpse of it one day and was struck by the enigmatic smile upon the lady's face. It seemed to me she was mocking all the courtiers who were bowing and scraping to have the privilege of handing Louis his handkerchief!"

"I wonder what other changes will she bear witness to?" mused Montesquieu.

Chapter 13

The Growth of Economic Bubbles

On Place Louis-le-Grand, where several financiers resided, John Law, a Scotsman, had taken up residence. Born into a wealthy banking family in Fife, Scotland, he had traveled to London and lived the good life. He developed an affection for Elizabeth Villers, which led to a duel with her intended, Edward Wilson. His triumph over that young man ended in a charge of murder commuted to a fine. When Wilson's family demanded he be incarcerated, he fled.

Having traveled widely and being conversant with the working of markets and monopolies, he settled in Paris. He felt his idea of creating a central bank that issued paper money, which could be bankrolled by the formation of a stock company, might be useful in France. One evening at a soirée hosted by a friend, he met Philippe d'Orléans, the Regent.

"Good evening, John. From what my friends tell me, you are an economist of rare talent."

"Thank you, Sire. Innovation based on observation of systems in England and the Netherlands, as well as an understanding of the basic workings of money, has been the focus of my life study."

"I confess, having just assumed care of the nation as Regent, we are in dire need of a solution to our financial woes. Wars are expensive. Would you be willing to discuss your ideas with our Banque Générale?" asked d'Orléans.

"Of course. And I have an acquaintance, an Englishman by the name of Thomas Pitt, who has recently returned from India. While there, he made an incredible and valuable purchase. I think it would interest you."

"Really, well I would be very happy to meet this gentleman. I will leave you to make the arrangements."

When the three met, d'Orléans was fascinated by Pitt's stories of the wealth being generated by England's overseas trade.

"John said you had a particular object for sale. May I see the item?"

"Indeed." Pitt reached into his jacket, took out a small velvet pouch and removed a ring.

"Oh my word!" Philippe just stared at the 141 carats diamond that glittered on its velvet cushion.

"C'est magnifique! Combien?"

"Shall we say 135,000 pounds?"

"Oui. I shall call it The Regent. It is exquisite!"

Law also met with members of the Banque Générale and he was successful in convincing them to establish a monopoly, the Mississippi Company, which would control the Louisiana Territory in the Americas. Shares would be sold and this would allow the government to issue paper money. Philippe made Law his Controller General of Finance. As the share price started to rise, more and more people from peasant to aristocrat bought them up. The rise came more from the demand, rather than the actual development of the area. Frenchmen were far more attached to their homeland and had far less desire to settle in distant colonies. The share price kept rising and inflation ensued. Some of the wiser investors converted their paper money to coin but soon the bubble burst and John Law was forced to flee Paris.

Ironically, while the French were in a frenzy of investing in a scheme touted as a sure thing, England was also caught up in the euphoria of a similar financial scheme. The same combination of ignorance and greed led many in England to buy shares in the South Sea Company. However, here, many should have known better. The government debt was to be financed through the South Sea Company being given a monopoly of foreign trade in South America. The Treaty of Utrecht had also granted England the asiento, which gave them the right to transport all Africans to Spanish and Portuguese colonies as well as the islands. Spain had put severe limits on other items that could be imported. Nevertheless, Englishmen rushed to buy shares, the price rose, the bubble burst.

Daniel Defoe sat with his friends reading the headlines of the *London Gazette*. "Fools. Every last one of them. The Spanish have been profiting from that trade for centuries. They weren't about to really share. There were only a few cities where we were permitted to open offices and could only send 500 tons to one of these offices each year. That's paltry."

"What's the asiento?" Josiah asked.

"It's the right to buy, transport, and sell Africans in the South Seas. Remember back when the Spanish Pope, Alexander VI, had to decide on the line of demarcation establishing Spanish and Portuguese rights to what was then unknown territory to the east and west of Europe, Spain had given the asiento to Portugal. During the War of Spanish Succession, France held the asiento and then it was transferred to us. Fundamentally, the slave trade pays off in cheap labor for those who buy, but the profit is not that great unless you are very efficient."

"Well I heard from my friends who worked for the company, the original so-called investors knew it wasn't worth much but they hyped it as this incredible opportunity and sold out when they had made a profit. They're just crooks."

"Those who lost weren't just the riff raff. I have a friend who works at the Mint. Even the great Sir Isaac Newton bought shares. He did sell them at a tidy profit, but the shares kept rising and the greedy fool bought in again and now he's lost a tidy fortune. Madness is what it is."

"Well, at least now Parliament will investigate and hopefully heads will roll. I understand that Robert Walpole was one who bought shares but sold at a profit." Looking at Defoe, he grinned and said, "Maybe those who lost out should join Robinson Caruso." The others chuckled at this reference to Defoe's recently published book of that name.

Chapter 14

The Birth of a Philosophe

François-Marie Arouet sat on the straw pallet within his windowless cell reflecting on his predicament. His lineage did not secure him a more comfortable abode with all the amenities. The Regent, Philippe d'Orléans, had taken umbrage at a verse that satirized Philippe's incestuous relationship with his daughter. Someone had told Philippe that Arouet was said to be the author. A *lettre de cachet* was issued. François reflected on the great plays of the Greeks that revolved around incestuous relationships. *Oedipus, how could you do it, kill your own father and marry your own mother! Of course you didn't know but does that excuse you?* His thoughts continued to wander. *Yes*, he smiled at the thought, *I shall rewrite Sophacles's tragedy into a love story and focus on virtue. I will be a writer even if my father disowns me!*

When Francois was released, he took his manuscript *Oedipe* to the manager of the Theatre Français.

"Arouet, nice to see you. I heard about your incarceration. You had best watch your satirical tongue. It would seem you have enemies in high places."

"Yes, indeed. However, my time was not wasted. I brought you a gift." François handed him the manuscript and saw the manager's brow furrow as he read the title page. *Oedipe* Tragedie pare Monsieur de Voltaire. He turned an enquiring gaze upon Arouet.

"*C'est mon nom de plume.*"

"I look forward to reading it. Will you be at the salon of the Duchesse du Maine?"

"*Mais certainment.* She is a delightful hostess and willing to receive a scoundrel such as myself, at least as long as I enliven the conversation!"

When *Oedipe* opened, it was highly acclaimed. Both the Duc d'Orléans and his daughter, the Duchesse du Berry, attended the premiere performance. They congratulated Voltaire on his work. *Am I the only one to see the irony?* thought Voltaire as their flattering comments wafted through his mind. Seeing the expressions on some of his friends' faces, he realized many had the same thought. Even his barbs at religion seemed to have gone unnoticed. His mind went to Jocasta's words, 'Our priests are not what a vain people believe; our credulity is the foundation of all their science.' Of course the viewer would equate such criticism to the gods of Greek mythology but maybe they would, given an opening, review their conception of the Church. Such musing led Voltaire to decide upon his next project, a poem he had begun while incarcerated about the first Bourbon king, Henry IV, who had stood for peace and religious toleration. When *Poème de la Ligue* was published, Voltaire wisely chose a publisher in Geneva and refrained from denoting authorship. Anonymity was not just the veil used by females! The ease with which a few of the middle class or minor nobility now mixed with the powerful aristocrats of the realm in the salons of Paris contributed to the rise in Voltaire's popularity.

Chapter 15

The Power of the Printed Word

War on the continent had been felt in a minimal way in America. In Boston, on the Charles River, young Ben Franklin escaped the confinement of his parents' two-bedroom apartment overcrowded with his many siblings. He would often lie on the grass on the bank of the Charles River reading used books someone had lent him or the few his father, Josiah, had in his small library. He loved Bunyan's work *Pilgrims Progress* and marveled at the great men of Greek and Roman history in Plutarch's *Lives*. When he was twelve, he was apprenticed to his older brother, James, who was the printer for the one newspaper in Boston, *The Boston Gazette*. Four years later, James set up his own paper, *The New England Courant*. While the work was hard and James a harsh taskmaster, Ben had access to more articles, letters, and used books, which he read deep into the night. He was determined to become a writer and used all that he read to practice the art of prose writing.

James Franklin knew that to be successful, he had to offer reading material that ran counter to the government's mouthpiece, *The Boston Gazette*. His first opportunity involved inoculation against small pox that Boston's leader, Cotton Mather, was encouraging.

"I've decided the public should be warned of this menace to their health. Dr. William Douglass, the only doctor in Boston with an actual medical degree, agrees and he will allow us to publish his letter of rebuttal," said James to his staff.

"I would be happy to lend a hand," said John Checkley with relish. "The Mathers are much too uppity! First they supported witch hunts and now this!" Ben didn't agree. He remembered back to Mather's *Bonifacius: Essays to Do Good,* which was very similar to Daniel Defoe's *An Essay Upon Projects.* Mather had changed. Ben lost track of the conversation as he focused on what made these works so satisfying. Progress. Yes, progress, making lives better. Ben looked up from his reverie and decided to keep his reservations to himself. If their paper found an audience, it would give him the opportunity to express his own ideas.

By opposing the government's stance on inoculation, James got the response he had hoped for since many of the inhabitants agreed that inoculation was dangerous. Circulation increased rapidly. One day, James arrived at the *Courant* office and unlocked the door. As had happened before, papers had been slid under the door. He picked them up. "What have we here. John, Thomas, have a read."

"What is it, hmmm, a letter by Silence Dogwood," said Thomas. He began to read and then looked up and smiled. "A woman expressing her views, I love it, sounds like my Aunt Mary. She's always saying what we all feel, criticizing the unlimited power of the clergy, the danger of arbitrary government."

"I love the style. It could have come from the pen of Addison or Steele in *The Spectator*."

Ben turned away to hide his smile of delight. If they only knew the hours I have spent studying and rewriting *Spectator* articles to improve my own writing! Each week, a new article by Silence Dogwood would appear and *The Courant's* readers loved it.

"Hey, guys, listen to this one on Increase Mather's Harvard. Essentially she's saying only those with riches shall enter the portals of learning, regardless of their lack of mental capacity. Too true!"

Week after week, a letter would appear on issues of civic improvement. Writing from the female point of view came easily to Ben. His favorite sibling was a younger sister and he saw no reason why women should not be educated as he found them to be just as capable of reasoning as any man. And, they were just as willing to defend such values as free speech and expose the hypocrisy of the Puritan government solidifying church and state into one. The only reason the state had not objected to the satiric attacks of Silence Dogwood was because she was a mere female. Thus, Ben's last entry was to confess that Silence Dogwood was a man! His brother had had suspicions and did not appreciate being upstaged by his little brother. Thus, James wrote an article on the hypocrisy of religion. The General Court was highly displeased and when James refused to bow to their censorship, they banished the paper. James went to serve a month in prison but before he left, he met with his staff.

"What are we going to do?" asked Thomas.

"I refuse to give in. Henceforth, *The Courant* will appear 'Printed and sold by Benjamin Franklin.'" Thus, *The Courant* survived but the relationship between Ben and James deteriorated.

"I've had it, I'm leaving," said Ben.

"But your indenture to James isn't up. Where will you go? What will you do?" asked his friend Ryan.

"Anywhere else. I'm sick of my brother's jealousy, total lack of appreciation, and beatings. It's not fair. I know every part of the printing business, even carried it alone for him, and I can write. He is just being mean in demanding five more years of my life as his apprentice. I'll go to New York or Philadelphia. They have papers. I'll find a way."

"What can I do to help?" asked Ryan.

"I need a ticket to New York. Here's the money to pay for it. Use another name." Thus, Ben Franklin left Boston in the fall of 1723.

* * *

On the opposite side of the world, when Kang'Xi, the Emperor of China, died in 1723, he was survived by fourteen sons. Over the years, it had been assumed that Yinreng, the crown prince, would be his successor. But Kang'Xi deposed him from this position. Then most thought Yinsi would take his place. Years passed and finally, as the end approached, he designated his fourth son, Yinzhen, his successor. Out of deference to his father, Yinzhen chose to live in the Hall of Mental Cultivation instead of the Palace of Heavenly Purity within Zijin Cheng, the Forbidden City. Yinzhen chose the era name Yongzheng. Yinzhen and his son, twelve year old Hongli, stood on the tower of the northwestern corner of the vast complex that made up the Forbidden City. Here the walls were bordered by a moat of water.

"Your grandfather, Kang'Xi, and I were always close. Due to circumstances, I was raised by my father and we shared mutual affection for each other and, for you, his grandson. He valued certain principles above all: honesty, harmony, responsibility for those under his care, and the demonstration of leadership skills. Quite frankly, the last is not one of my strongest suits as I never expected to be chosen but I know he saw them all in you. We will make it very clear that you will be my successor. You must apply yourself in all areas to prepare yourself to be deserving of such a privilege. I shall make you Prince Bao of the First Rank. There are many who will contend my elevation and I will have to play one against the other."

Chapter 16

Peter's Vision Realized

Peter's wife, Catherine, and Alex Menshikov's wife, Darya, were sharing a quiet moment overlooking the incredible water fountains at Peterhof created by Mikhail Kazlovsky. Peter had constructed this lavish retreat to be closer to his favorite project, the naval fortress, Kronstadt.

"Peter is an unusual man," said Darya. "On an individual basis, he only cares about loyalty and merit; he rewards those who, in some way, contribute to helping create his vision for Russia's future. Yet, he seems oblivious to the suffering of the serfs under the Russian nobility. And his rages! His son by Eudoxia, Alexis, was a fool to try to escape his responsibilities and flee to Vienna. I don't blame the Senate for cutting him from the line of succession but his punishment was so severe the he had an apoplectic fit. I don't think Peter shed a tear when Alexis died. I don't know how you can calm him down when no one else can. He's lucky to have you," said Darya.

"Thank you, Darya. Peter is driven, sometimes by demons. The physical and mental anguish he suffers is very real. He brought me from nothing to not only marriage but he tells me he wants to make me Empress. Frankly, it all seems slightly unreal," Catherine confessed.

"Well, the world will never know, but you may have saved his empire. Remember after Poltava, when Peter insisted on pursuing Charles XII into Ottoman territory and we were caught by the Sultan's

Grand Vizier at Pruth? Shafirov said that you supported Peter's peace offer to Baltadji and even agreed to throw in all your jewels if he agreed to our retreat. Had he followed the Sultan's orders, all would have been lost. Poltava would have been meaningless," said Darya.

"As flattered as I am and although I did make such an offer, Baltadji agreed to our release based on his own desire to end hostilities." Catherine smiled to herself thinking back to their subsequent trip to Europe in 1717. They had been well received in all of the courts. Her reminiscing was interrupted by the arrival of Abram Petrovich Gannibal whom Catherine warmly welcomed. Abram's ebony skin denoted his African heritage. Islamic control of the east African coast had melded with the local peoples and produced its own language, Swahili. As often happened, the Ottoman Sultans kept sons of African chiefs of the interior as surety that trade would not be interrupted. Russia's Ambassador to the Ottoman court had purchased Abram and presented him to Peter. He became Peter's valet and godson and was treated as a family member spending his free hours playing as a child with Catherine's daughters, Anne and Elizabeth.

"We have missed you. You must share your adventures in Paris," said Catherine.

"As I have missed all of you," said Gannibal as he sat down on the brocade couch. "When in Metz, I expanded my education but study is no substitute for reality so as you know, I joined the French army and enrolled in the royal artillery academy at La Fère. I thought it would please my dear godfather, Peter. We were engaged in Louis XV's confrontation with his uncle in Spain, Philip V. I was promoted to captain so it seemed appropriate to have a surname, thus, I chose the great general Hannibal," he smiled mischievously. "Now I hope to serve my dear master, Peter, as a military engineer. He has been so kind and I am happy to repay his trust in me."

"And did you enjoy Paris?" asked Darya.

"Yes, indeed. I met a delightful young man, Francois d'Arouet, a playwright and poet who was very witty and a popular figure with the Duchesse du Maine at Sceaux. He has assumed a pen name, Voltaire, so although I'm not a writer, I have used my creative side in choosing an appropriate surname, Gannibal."

"You will be amazed at the growth of the educational opportunities here; Peter has founded schools for navigation, artillery, languages, medicine, engineering and plans one for science although we still have to depend upon foreign instructors, it is a great start. And, we now have our own newspaper, *Vedomosti*," said Catherine.

At that moment, Elizabeth, her father, and Alex Menshikov joined them on the terrace. Abram rose and smiled with enthusiasm as they came forward. Although Elizabeth was now fourteen, they had been good friends before Abram had left for France. Alex's smile was not quite as welcoming as he resented Abram's foreign birth and superior education. However, he held his peace as Peter liked the young man. The lad had accompanied them on many a campaign. But now he was a man and Alex felt a potential adversary in influencing the Tsar. Nevertheless, he was honest enough to acknowledge to himself that Peter was a man of his own mind. When the last head of the Russian Orthodox Church died, Peter had essentially turned the Church into a department of the government by creating the Holy Synod. And, his Table of Ranks rewarded loyalty and merit, not birth and privilege.

"Any news from the east?"

"Unfortunately, the Chinese were not inclined to trade. We have not as yet heard back from Bering as to whether there is a land connection with America."

* * *

Peter Romanov died two years later and would be remembered as Peter the Great. Catherine became the Empress of Russia and would rule for two years, aided by Alex Menshikov. When she died, Alexis's son, Peter, was chosen as tsar because Menshikov knew that many of the boyars would not agree to Peter and Catherine's eldest daughter, Anne. Menshikov thought he would continue in power since Peter was only twelve. However, Peter II died five years later. The Dolgoruky and the Miloslavsky clans of Peter's stepmother, Maria, reasserted themselves and demanded that the next Tsar of Russia would be the line of Ivan V who had ruled as co-tsar with Peter. Thus, Anne, the second daughter of Ivan was selected. Menshikov's fall from favor was fast and hard. He lost his offices and decorations and was exiled to an estate in Siberia.

Chapter 17

Voltaire Discovers Reason

Voltaire was furious. He stood before the Warden in the Bastille. "*Je ne le crois pas!* The Chevalier de Rohan insulted me! Why do you honor the *lettre de cachet* and imprison me when he is the vile toad who set his lackeys upon me!"

"*Mais*, M. Voltaire, he is the Chevalier de Rohan," said the Warden.

"So what! Aside from a noble title what has he done? Nothing! He has the intelligence of a flea. Respect should be based on intellect, competence, and contribution."

The Warden secretly agreed but could do nothing. Voltaire, having vented his anger and frustration continued, "I know you are blameless. A favor. Could you please ask the Magistrate to meet with me?"

"Certainly, I shall be happy to ask him," said the Warden as he turned and left.

Voltaire mulled over the idea that had entered his head. Who knew how long he would have to sit behind these walls. No. He would bargain for a different punishment. When he met with the Magistrate, he offered to go into voluntary exile in England. This was acceptable to the court officials and so Voltaire departed for London.

Voltaire arrived in England in 1726 under myriad disadvantages. He did not speak English, his work was unknown across the channel, he had no wealth, and few friends. However, he did have the backing of Lord Bolingbroke who had, when he was ousted from the government in England, visited Paris. They had met in one of the salons and Bolingbroke had given him a letter of introduction so that he would be well received in London. Within six months he had overcome all obstacles. He sought out the equivalent of the salon in France. In London, he was invited to the Scriblerus Club.

"M. Voltaire, I am so pleased that you could join us. May I present my friend and visiting guest, Jonathan Swift," said Alexander Pope.

"Enchanted to meet you. I found your work, *Gulliver's Travels* extremely diverting. A satire on the human condition is a universal connector free of cultural barriers."

"Well, I have found the powers that be seem moribund in devising a rational system and now, those who I would support have fallen from power and we now have a king who does not even speak our language," said Swift.

"Although you may feel constraints, what strikes me most is your freedom of speech, the ability to express your ideas even if they are dissonant to some of your leaders. In my land, one must always be wary of what one says. All works must be approved by Government or Church censors," commented Voltaire.

"That explains Montesquieu's *Lettres Persanes* that a friend of mine sent me. He distances himself from views expressed by making them come from the mouths of foreigners."

"That's how Thomas More wrote *Utopia* when his king, Henry VIII, would punish criticism of his rule."

"Tell me M. Voltaire, what have you written?"

"A play, *Oedipe* and poems," said Voltaire. "Perhaps you have heard of *Le Henriade*? I believe that is how you call it here, in England."

"Have you met my friend John Gay? He's working on a piece called *The Beggar's Opera*. A whole host of villains and rogues."

Voltaire also spent a good deal of time in Drury Lane. He was fascinated by the plays of Shakespeare. Although popular in England for over a century, their circulation on the continent had not followed. The French court had continued with French favorites like Molière, Racine, and Corneille. Voltaire was amazed at the difference. French tragedies were the deliverance of the storyline through oration while Shakespeare used actors who acted out the emotions and there were even moments of drollery in the most serious themes. The spontaneity and emotions evoked were far more stimulating than French plays. William Chetwood, a friend of Voltaire, would provide a prompt copy so that as Voltaire's artistic sense was inspired, his mastery of English was perfected.

Voltaire also met prominent Whigs through a merchant, Everard Fawkener. These Whig intellectuals greatly admired the works of Locke and Newton. Although he never actually met Newton, Voltaire was an assiduous student of all of his works as they were not allowed to circulate in France as some of his ideas contradicted those of René Descartes. Exposure to natural philosophy transformed him, especially his contemplation of the Newtonian belief that God was the creator but science was there to explain his creation; that reason, human reasoning, was the key to understanding.

In 1729, Voltaire was allowed to return to France. Shortly after his departure, another Frenchman, Baron de Montesquieu, visited England. What interested him the most about English society was the emerging form of government. He admired the separation of powers between the king and Parliament that limited the concentration of power of one individual, the king. However, he knew as well as Voltaire, that such ideas would be anathema in France.

In Paris, Voltaire was again welcomed back by his friends. A few of them met at the home of Charles de la Condamine before going to the salon for the evening.

"We have missed you. And how was your stay in England?"

"*Incroyable*! Very different from here, I assure you. It is a much freer society. I found much to admire."

"Well, I do hope you will write up your experiences,"

"And spend more time in the Bastille? No, thank you."

They all laughed but knew it was all too true.

"How are your finances?" asked Charles.

"Why do you ask?" replied Voltaire.

"Well, I have an idea. The government is sponsoring another lottery. After Law's catastrophe, not to mention d'Orléans' wasteful spending, they are in need of funds but this one is flawed and I know how we can take advantage of the flaw."

"You're sure?"

"Yes."

"Count me in," said Voltaire.

Voltaire's gamble paid off. His share of the profit set him up for life. In addition, the government now saw fit to release the funds from his father's estate. He was incredibly fortunate to have this financial independence as most of his fellow philosophes had to rely on patrons who could be very fickle. Now he focused on building up his public stature by turning out poems, plays, and essays that circulated in the salons. He was even allowed to reside with the royal court at Versailles! It was here that he became re-acquainted with Émilie du Châtelet.

Émilie's father, the Baron de Breteuil, was a most unusual man. He actually allowed and encouraged his daughter to study Greek, Latin, Italian, German, mathematics and science. In addition, he would have her join the men who came to his salon every Thursday evening, which is where she had first met Voltaire. However, as was the custom, her marriage was arranged. Fortunately, she and her husband were mutually tolerant of any side affairs that might occur. She had entered into correspondence with famed economists and scientists and had many friends at the Academy of Science that met at the Louvre. Many of these gentlemen would congregate at Gradeau's coffeehouse for further discussion. Again, women were excluded. So donning men's wear, she entered and her warm welcome induced the proprietor to cast a blind eye on this new member. When she returned to court and became re-acquainted with Voltaire, their relationship developed into one of real affection and admiration for the other's intellect.

One day, as they strolled through the gardens of Versailles, they were conversing about his current project, *Lettres Philosophiques*, which was based on his travels to England and immersion in the scientific community. The result had been to turn him into a Deist. They were now engaged in a collaborative conversation on his rejection of organized religion.

"Where did religion originate? Basically from ignorance. A futile attempt to ward off violent eruptions that seemed to destroy lives at random. It was easy to equate misery with some malevolent force. Thus, the desire to propitiate such an evil spirit and then to construct an invisible all knowing being who held ultimate power. Then some enterprising soul, desiring the power to control, claimed to speak for this invisible power *et voila*, religion was born," said Voltaire.

"Don't forget the embellishment that solidified control, the concept of eternity. Life is but a fleeting moment but eternity is forever. Thus, the multitude was convinced that their destitute wretched lives would miraculously improve in heaven as long as they abided by the script the synagogue, church, or mosque provided," said Émilie.

"The growth of religion stunted man's intellect. All was attributed to God's will. All was his creation. But today we have discovered reason and the more we engage in intellectual exploration and experimentation, the need for religion fades. God set nature in motion but it is up to us to divine its secrets. As our understanding grows, so will our happiness. But, I caution you never underestimate the power of the Church to continue its control of the ignorant masses," said Voltaire.

"That's true but even long ago, in ancient Greece, some like Socrates questioned the concept of a hereafter. For him, the possibility of everlasting peace in one final sleep or something beyond were equal. He feared neither result. However, the Church today depicts excruciating results, popularized by Dante, and accepted as truth."

"But Socrates felt such peace because he believed he had never relinquished his search for the truth. I have often noted that small children seem to have an innate sense of fairness. Their parents teach moral precepts which make them aware of right and wrong in their society but if we were to self determine, I'm sure that if a parent does or says something that the child feels is just wrong, that is God within us, guiding us. However, when faced with real decisions as we age, we ignore that inner voice too often. Socrates did not ignore it. Just because it has been corrupted doesn't mean that He doesn't exist. We are just emerging from our ignorance of his creation, nature in all its glory."

"What saddens me the most," said Émilie in a more critical tone, "is that the more people follow the admonishments of their religious leaders, the more they are deflected from having to solve problems in a practical way. The Church and monarchs have a symbiotic relationship. Look at Louis XIV's 'divine' kingship. And others imitate him."

"Well, it seems to me that there are too few who actually improve the lives of the masses. Their sycophants may acquire wealth and power but the vast majority are just used and discarded. That is why I wrote *Le Henriade*. Henry IV was one of the few who at least tried to ameliorate the suffering of his people, recognizing the danger of civil war and religious zealotry."

"What if we all believed that we only have a lifetime on earth? That there was no afterlife? Why would we all then not strive to make the most of the life we were given? Why would we put up with the corrupt leaders and not insist that they solve problems and assure protection of each and every person? Then, each could pursue their own happiness."

"How would you define 'happiness'?"

"Happiness means fulfillment. To focus on that which gives your life meaning. To earn a degree and practice law, to paint or write stories, to till the earth and reap the benefits. To stay true to your values. As Aristotle said, to correct our faults and become the best that we can be. But, so few are free. They labor for others, not for themselves. A few have property and indulge their senses but that does not ensure that they will find happiness."

Chapter 18

The Desire to Improve Lives

When young Ben Franklin left Boston, he found no opening in the printing trade in New York. However, being a gregarious, honest soul and having more personal magnetism that most, he had impressed William Bradford, the printer of the *New York Gazette,* who suggested Ben try Philadelphia where Bradford's son had a shop. Although the son, Andrew Bradford, did not need additional help, another printer, Samuel Keimer, did. Ben found a room to rent with the Read family and set to work on his future. With determination, he set forth to improve his skills and develop contacts in Philadelphia.

There had been setbacks but finally, by dint of hard work and a deserved reputation for such, Ben found a backer for opening his own shop. His sponsor, Governor William Keith, was a benevolent soul who, unfortunately for Ben, was not always able to fulfill his promises. He had offered to loan Ben the money to buy printing equipment in London. However, the promised letters of credit never arrived on board the ship Ben was taking to London. By the time Ben realized that they were not coming, the ship had begun its voyage. When he arrived in London, he found work at Samuel Palmer's print shop in order to pay for his return ticket. Franklin made friends easily and one, a fellow American by the name of Thomas Denham, whom he had met on the passage over, offered to pay his way back to Philadelphia and the two planned to open a dry goods store.

Unfortunately, shortly after they returned to Philadelphia, Denham died and so Ben went back to work at Keimer's.

Franklin's luck finally turned when a co-worker, Hugh Meredith, said his father would set them up in their own print shop. At last, he was in control and set to work with his usual diligence. Franklin's circle of friends expanded and several of them helped Ben form a club where together, one evening a week, they would gather to discuss a variety of topics. They called themselves The Leather Apron Club or the Junto, for short.

"Have any of you read Defoe's *Essay on Projects*?"

"I read *Robinson Caruso*," offered George Webb. "Jolly good story."

"Yes, it was a fine tale. But I'm referring to another work, one to improve the lives of all the people. England and the Government appointees do nothing but ensure that trade continues to enrich the mother country. There is no attention given to our needs," said Ben.

"What exactly do you mean?" asked Thomas Godfrey.

"We need basics: paving bricks for the streets, constables to patrol, a fire department. Volunteers could fill some of these positions, but for the rest we could ask the legislature to levy a small tax to pay for them. Everyone would benefit."

"I'm in, where do you want to start?"

"Well, first, many writers have contributed ideas on how best to pursue this agenda so what we need is a circulating library. Even if we had a bookstore, few can afford the purchase price. But, all of us have used books we could contribute. Cotton Mather's *Bonifacius or Essays to Do Good* was inspiring to me in seeing myself in a community that took responsibility for the welfare of their fellow citizens."

"And you have this on spectral evidence, I suppose," said Hugh Meredith. The others laughed at Hugh's reference to the witch trials over thirty years before.

"Times have changed in so many ways. The population has grown; merchants compete with landowners. There are many poor who deserve a helping hand."

"I agree," said William Coleman, "I'm in." The others nodded their assent.

Ben's paper, *The Pennsylvania Gazette* thrived. He was also fortunate to become the legislature's printer. Articles were informative but also enlivened by gossip that kept the tone light. Readership steadily grew. Many of the Letters to the Editor were written by Ben himself to express contrary points of view. His disciplined attitude toward his own conduct was now second nature and the community benefitted enormously. In *Poor Richard's Almanac*, he would include the usual information but used it as a vehicle to instruct and entertain the common folk. His pithy proverbs spread rapidly. Sales of the almanac made him a wealthy man.

* * *

During this period, America would add a new colony, Georgia. James Oglethorp initiated the project. He was a Tory MP for Godalming in Surrey, not far from London. His life reflected that of the gentry living off the rent of his estates. He had studied at Oxford but left to attend a military academy in France and then joined Prince Eugene of Savoy against the Turks. When he returned to England, he followed the Oglethorpe tradition of serving in Parliament. In 1729, he was exposed to a totally different world when he learned of a friend's death in Fleet Prison. His friend, Robert Castell, had fallen into debt and was committed to Fleet

Prison where he had died of smallpox. The more Oglethorpe learned of the circumstances, the more horrified he became and demanded Parliament hold an inquiry into the conditions and management of the prison. In February, Oglethorpe and other members of the Gaols Committee visited Fleet Prison.

"This is utterly appalling. Not being able to pay a debt or going bankrupt does not deserve this punishment. This place is filthy, the prisoners are clearly underfed and close to starvation, and many have open running sores," said John Percival.

"It would appear that the warden, Thomas Bambridge, puts the screws on them all to pay, pay, pay. That's ridiculous, considering they're here because they couldn't pay their debts," said Archibald Grant.

"I can't believe what Sir William Rich told us about his treatment of being kept in irons, burned with a red-hot poker, and locked in that small dark room that is referred to as the Strong Room. It's worse than any dungeon I've ever seen. The filth is nauseating and the stench unbearable. This is murder by slow agonizing torture. We must stop it!" said Oglethorpe.

"Someone told me that another prisoner, Solas, a Portuguese, was kept in the dungeon, shackled and starving for two months. He is clearly in terror of Bambridge, as are they all," said Grant. "It may be difficult to get testimony."

A member of their party kept slightly aside from the group, sketching scenes of all that the committee was witnessing. The look on his face was inscrutable. He was an engraver, William Hogarth, who had, from an early age, sketched the everyday life of the people of London. He had never told anyone that his father had been incarcerated in this very prison for five long years. He was determined to expose the folly, injustice, and pure stupidity of life in all spheres of English society.

As Oglethorpe returned to his estate, he reflected back on the session of Parliament. Bambridge had been charged with murder and extortion. Although all were too terrified to testify on the murder charge, he was convicted of gross extortion and sentenced to Newgate Prison. The stupidity of sending debtors to prison seemed so obvious. Yes, those who had friends with money and influence were allowed, for a sum, to work during the day and return at night but the vast majority were at the mercy of alms, which clearly provided little. There had to be a better solution. Oglethorpe reflected back to the case of William Penn who had founded the colony of Pennsylvania. Penn was an admirable human being who should have been venerated but, because of the evil avarice of his agent Philip Ford and his conniving wife, Penn, in his later years, fell deeply in debt and was to be sent to Fleet Prison. Fortunately, this was converted to house arrest and then Queen Anne forgave his debt. What if there were some way debtors could start over?

Oglethorpe came up with an answer to this question. He petitioned King George II for a charter to build a colony in America whereby such debtors could start over. In 1732, a charter was granted to Oglethorpe and twenty other trustees but the king and most of the trustees saw the colony only as a buffer between the entrenched Spanish in St. Augustine and the prosperous colonies of the Carolinas. Thus, when the first colonists left in November of 1732, none of the 114 were debtors but were basically poor artisans. Each male would receive the same amount of land and modest housing as large holdings were forbidden as was slavery. Oglethorpe gave up his comfortable life and went with them.

Chapter 19

Freedom of the Press Challenged

In New York City, the English appointed governor, Cosby, was causing anger to rise among the colonial population. "I'm fed up with the Governor's arbitrary and self-serving judgments. He had no excuse for dismissing Chief Justice Morris. He did it because Morris had published his dissent in the decision reached in the Cosby v. Van Dam case. Morris felt he had no right to even bring such a case, which dealt with an equity issue as the court that heard the case had no jurisdiction. Only Parliament has the power to create such a court. It's time to expose his tyranny," said William Smith. His partner, James Alexander, nodded in agreement.

"You're right, William. William Bradford's *New York Gazette* supports Governor Cosby. But, readers have the right to know the abuses he perpetrates. We are all treated as second-class citizens. I'm a lawyer and can verify Morris's decision in Cosby v. Van Dam was legitimate. The English who seek appointments here don't care about us; they just want to feather their nests. Let's start our own paper."

Thus, a second paper appeared in New York City, the *New York Weekly Journal*. Needless to say, public exposure and mockery of Gov. Cosby came as an affront and he determined to stop its publication. Perhaps because James Alexander and William Smith were such well-respected attorneys, Cosby chose to prosecute their printer, John Peter Zenger, on charges of seditious libel. Although two separate grand juries were convened, much to Cosby's chagrin, they refused to indict.

"I don't believe it. That fool Cosby is now asking the Assembly to have a public hangman burn issues of our paper!" said Smith.

"Does the Governor think he is the Pope that he would order such a ridiculous action? He's only hurting himself."

Cosby wouldn't give up. He then circumvented the need of a Grand Jury indictment by a highly disliked legal procedure known as 'information,' whereby a grand jury indictment was unnecessary. His Attorney General filed an 'information' before the Supreme Court and two of Cosby's allies in the Court issued a bench warrant for Zenger's arrest. The publishers, Alexander and Smith, went to their printer's defense. Their opening argument targeted the legitimacy of the appointment to the Supreme Court and, thus, its right to bring an information suit. In retaliation for such, the two men were struck from the list of attorneys admitted to practice before the New York Supreme Court! Zenger, still in jail, asked the court to appoint a lawyer. Thus, John Chambers, young and newly admitted to practice law, was so appointed to defend Zenger.

Zenger's wife, Anna, was discussing her husband's chances with James Alexander and William Smith.

"Now what? I refuse to give up," said Anna.

"Well, quite honestly, Chambers, by twice challenging the list of jurors, has ensured that they are not biased against your husband," said William. "News of the case has spread. We must see if we can find a more experienced attorney, outside of New York and Cosby's power who can help Chambers."

"Actually, I may know just the man. Andrew Hamilton. I will write to him and see if he would be willing to assist in the case," said Alexander.

Hamilton did agree to assist on the case. Chambers agreed to his appearing in court on Zenger's behalf. Thus, the trial opened on August 4th, 1735, and Chambers entered a plea of not guilty. He described the case, said the Attorney General had to prove who was responsible for the alleged libel, and ended by stating that the Attorney General would not be able to provide such proof. Andrew Hamilton then rose and spoke as a defense witness for Zenger. He stated Zenger had printed the journals but saw nothing in what he was asked to print as being untruthful. He went on to urge the jurors to consider the truth and he urged them to see the broader scope, the inquiry as liberty. Zenger was found not guilty. The concept of a free press was forever embedded in the American identity.

Chapter 20

Inventions to Improve Lives

In various hamlets in England, the steadily growing demand for clothe was met by the development of 'cottage industry.' During the evenings and winter months, local peasants would perform specific tasks. An agent would supply wool, which would first be carded. He then transported the carded wool to other cottages where it was spun into thread. Then he took the thread to other cottages where it was woven into strips of cloth. While this putting-out system added to the peasants' income, it was often frustrating to the agent when an order had not been completed on time or the quality of workmanship was not uniform. Some men worked on a regular basis in what came to be called a factory where the frames could be larger. The frames had horizontal and vertical reeds that separated warp from weft; the warp was vertical, the weft was horizontal. The thread was attached to a shuttle whereby one man pushed it across the frame as far as he could and then another man, standing on the opposite side of the loom, would pull it the rest of the way and then return it.

Back in 1718, John Kay of Bury in Lancashire, went to work for a loom reed maker. The reeds used came from tall plants found in the wetlands. His mother was surprised when John returned to their small farm a month after he had left.

"I have mastered the trade and, I have a great idea," he said.

"And just what is it?" asked his mother with a skeptical look.

"Let me experiment and then I will show you."

The next day, John visited the town's master metalworker, Samuel, and placed an order for wire. He watched in fascination as the metal was annealed or heated to make it malleable. Samuel tapered one end and inserted it in the hole in the draw plate. Gently he pulled it through with tongs and then gently flattened it. When the required amount was made, John went home and commandeered his mother's small loom. He removed all of the reeds and replaced them with the metal wires.

"There, it's finished. Come see." His mother and brother William looked at the loom.

"Don't you see? Reeds only work for a short time; they constantly crack or break. But, by using metal wires they will last forever. Think of all the looms in England!"

The practicality of his innovation was recognized and he was able to support himself by making the wire and fitting it to existing looms throughout England. He returned to Bury and put his mind to other improvements. He patented another of his machines, which corded and twisted wool and flax to make worsted. This was followed by another invention, which he called a wheeled shuttle, that allowed the weft to pass through the warp threads much more rapidly and allowed for greater loom width. The wheeled shuttle flew to the opposite side of the loom and back. No longer did a second attendant have to stand on the opposite side to return the shuttle. *Weavers will love it*, he thought. He sought out a partner to make the flying-shuttle as most referred to it, in Colchester, Essex. Those who ran larger production factories were enthusiastic. It speeded up the weaving process. However, weaver employees were not pleased. It would eliminate jobs. They protested and Kay's attempts to get a patent and have his invention used became tied up in the courts. Nevertheless, he continued perfecting his invention.

* * *

In Barrow, Yorkshire, close to the seaport of Hull, John Harrison learned the trade of carpentry from his father. He became very familiar with the differing properties of wood imported from all parts of the world. John seemed born to observe, reflect, and internalize to accommodate his incredible curiosity. A visiting clergyman took note of John's desire to learn and loaned him his manuscript copy of Nicholas Saunderson's *Lectures on Natural Philosophy*. Over the ensuing months and then years, John had mastered the laws of motion. This led him to absorb Newton's *Principia*. Seeking a practical application for the scientific principles, John built a pendulum clock. Most of the internal parts were carved from wood. Now he had a second occupation and his clocks were so admired that he was hired to build a tower clock for Sir Charles Pelham's manor in Brocklesby Park.

"Good morning, John, how is work progressing?" asked Sir Charles.

"It's going well, Sir," replied John.

"Frankly, I'm surprised so many internal parts are made of wood. Will they last?"

"Yes, Sir. For instance, oak is incredibly strong. Or take the lignum vitae. This is a tropical hardwood that actually lubricates itself. Your clock will never need to be oiled. Metals expand and contract with climate change throwing the clock off and metal rusts. Plus, wood is lighter. However, for those few parts where I must use metal, I use brass."

"And the pendulum?"

"There I have used two different metals that counteract each other's expansion with temperature changes. Thus, it will, unlike other clocks, never be too fast or too slow."

"Amazing. Tell me, have you ever considered how your clock might be modified to be used at sea to determine longitude?" asked Pelham.

"When in Hull, I have heard sailors lament the lack of such a device. Many an accident might have been avoided if they could tell how far east or west their craft had travelled. It would be an intriguing challenge," said Harrison thoughtfully.

"Well, back in 1714, Queen Anne established a Board of Longitude which sponsored a contest for such an invention. The Board was to test and evaluate applications. As far as I know, no one has put forth any real possibility. It's a big prize for whoever does figure it out. Twenty thousand pounds for first prize. Well, I'm off to London. I appreciate your conscientious perfectionism."

"Thank you, Sir. The tower should be finished within the year."

John and his brother, James, knew that their clocks were more accurate than the reputedly best clockmakers in London. *But, to do it on land was far easier than on a rough sea,* John thought. *Standard pendulums would never work. But, what if it were like a seesaw, self-contained, and able to counter balance extreme seas?* Over the next few years, Harrison continued to mentally explore this idea. Finally, having written a detailed prospectus, he set off to find the only member that he had heard of who was on the Board of Longitude, Edmond Halley. Thus, he went to the Royal Observatory at Greenwich. It was a fortunate choice because Halley was one of the few scientific intelligentsia not puffed up by his own conceit. He was attentive to Harrison's explanation of the drawings he had brought.

"Very interesting. However, I'm an astronomer and have spent my life viewing and recording the heavens. We, too, have been trying to solve the same problem. Galileo was able to observe the moons of Jupiter, calculating and recording the orbital periods of these moons as well as their disappearance behind the giant planet. He had worked out far better reckoning of longitude, at least on land. Maps, since then, have been redrawn using this lunar model. Astronomers and mathematicians continue to try to figure out how to apply it to the sea." Halley paused, his brow creased. He remembered back to Isaac Newton's dismissal of the possibility of ever making a device that would work. "What we need is for a watchmaker to evaluate your idea and give it legitimacy from a source all on the Board consider an expert. I don't mean to offend but they're a rather top lofty set. Now, go and see George Graham and let's see what he has to say."

John realized the truth of this. He was, to them, a lowly artisan. *But, what if Graham stole his idea? What other choice do I have?* he thought.

At 10:00 in the morning, the butler opened the door to the Graham residence. John felt acutely uncomfortable but squared his shoulders and asked to see Mr. Graham. Soon that gentleman came into the entrance foyer. When he saw Harrison, his face turned more stern and he asked the reason for his visit.

"I have developed plans for a clock that can be used at sea to determine longitude," John replied stoutly.

"Really, you, a mere peasant, artisan, whatever, have developed the intricate mechanical theory and have solved this incredible problem that has puzzled the greatest minds for generations? Please, don't waste my time any further. Simon, please show Mr. Harrison out."

But John wouldn't give up. "Yes, Sir, I have. You can see it for yourself."

"I'm sorry young man, but I have more important matters to attend to."

"Why won't you even take a look? It solves the problem! If Edmond Halley felt it had merit, you can at least look at my plans," said Harrison heatedly.

He has a point, thought Graham. "Very well, come, set them on the table and I shall take a look."

Harrison stood silently, taking in the rich furnishings and feeling envious of the multitude of books that sat on shelves on either side of the fireplace. Meanwhile, Graham silently read, page after page. "Oh my word," he muttered. He read on to the last page. "Incredible. I think it actually might work. Come sit down." The two lost track of time, immersed in their discussion. Dinner was announced and Graham invited Harrison to share it with his family. Evening fell, and when Harrison prepared to leave, Graham insisted he take a loan so that he could devote his attention to making the machine he had envisioned. The two parted as best of friends.

Years would pass before Harrison was able to physically produce the first sea clock. In 1735, he put the four foot square clock in a wagon he had borrowed and returned to Graham's residence to show him the results of his labor. Graham then arranged for the clock to be seen by members of the Royal Society where Edmond Halley and others were very impressed. Graham wrote an enthusiastic endorsement for Harrison to present to the Board of Longitude. After much delay, Harrison was authorized to take it on the H.M.S. *Centurion* under Captain Proctor, who was bound for Lisbon. John was not a seaman and was seasick most of the way. Unfortunately, Captain Proctor died in Lisbon and had not recorded the success of H1 as the device was called. However, another ship was found to bring Harrison and his clock back to England. Captain Wills of the

H.M.S. *Orford* complied but Mother Nature lengthened the return with intermittent gales and calms. When land was sighted, Wills assumed it was Start on the coast of Dartmouth.

"No," insisted Harrison. "It is not Start. We are 60 miles further west."

"You're sure?" asked Wills somewhat dubiously.

"Positive." Wills looked at his map and said, "In that case, that must be what we call the Lizard on the Penzance peninsula." H1 was proven correct and Wills wrote an enthusiastic endorsement letter, which led to the convening of the Board of Longitude. When it met, almost all of those attending were clearly willing to have John do a trial run to the West Indies as was called for in the original Longitude Act. They believed Harrison had solved the problem. But John's mind was always churning. His desire was to create the perfect machine. On the voyage to Lisbon he had noted small defects even though no one else had noticed them. And, he pondered, how to make it smaller so that it didn't take up most of the Captain's cabin. Harrison wouldn't accept the 20,000 pounds until it was perfect. The Board was happy to grant him 250 pounds as seed money to be matched by the same amount when he brought in the new machine for its trial voyage.

Chapter 21

Fleeing Censorship

Having re-established himself in Paris, Voltaire finished *Letters on England*. Inevitably, the book dealt with the scientific and political changes of Newton and Locke, medical acceptance of inoculation for smallpox, and the freedom of expression. He had submitted it to the censors and waited impatiently for permission to publish it.

"What do you mean you saw a copy?" asked Voltaire.

"I did, *Lettres Philosophiques*," replied the Marquis du Châtelet.

"But, I haven't received approval from the royal censors. My publisher had no right to release it."

"Well, it's done," said Émilie. "We'll just have to wait and see how the authorities respond."

When Voltaire got news of the public burning of his book by the official hangman no less, he knew his arrest was imminent. He had no intention of a return visit to the Bastille.

"You must go to our estate at Cirey. If the authorities do pursue you with a *lettre de cachet*, you can easily slip across the nearby border into Lorraine, an independent province. However, we have some influence over Louis XV and will use it so you will not be pursued."

Émilie du Châtelet accompanied Voltaire to Cirey and then returned to Paris. After the authorities' tempers cooled, Voltaire had every intention of returning there as well. The château was rarely used and had fallen into disrepair. It sat upon a hill overlooking the countryside. At the base of the hill was an old picturesque moat. Trees dotted the hillside and birds lent music to his ear. As the days passed, he fell in love with his surroundings and decided to stay permanently. The first order of business was to set about repairs. Then, as he invited guests, he added another wing to accommodate them. And, what he wanted most finally came. Émilie returned, loved the changes that he had made, and agreed to stay permanently. The salon they established lured many to visit and enjoy extended stays. Voltaire's reputation as the leading *philosophe* continued to grow. Unlike most of the salons in Paris, Voltaire and Émilie were equally involved. Their love of Newtonian science led them to build a laboratory and experiment in the nature of fire. They encouraged each other in their writing and their partnership would prove productive.

Chapter 22

Fathers and Sons

"I'm leaving! I'm fed up with his abuse. I despise him! He'll never let me be me!" declared Frederick. His mother, Sophia Dorothea, and his sister, Wilhelmine, commiserated with his anguished outburst.

"Darling, I know he seems harsh at times. It's strange how the generations of Hohenzollerns are always at odds. Your great-grandfather, Frederick William, the Great Elector, turned Prussia into a militarized state. Although our lands are scattered far and wide within Europe, he forced all to contribute and support his military. His son, Frederick I, loved the arts and entertainment, which his father despised, so they, too, were always at odds. Your father despised everything Frederick I did to beautify the palaces, to bring learning and culture to Prussia. Your father is the one who packed up the Amber Room and sent it off to Peter, the Tsar of Russia." Sophia Dorothea's face was one of despair as she shared his feeling of loathing for her husband despite having multiple pregnancies as part of her duty as Queen.

Wilhelmine was very fond of her brother and said, "But what will you do?"

"I don't know. I'll think of something."

Mother and daughter cast each other glances that shared the same feeling of foreboding. Their feeling was justified when shortly thereafter, Frederick William I's angry voice was heard ordering that his son and Hans von Katte be stopped in their attempted flight to England and taken to Küstrin Fortress. "How dare he. It's obscene. This is treason!" On and on he ranted. Apparently, Frederick and Hans as well as a few other officers who had foolishly accompanied Frederick, were to be executed. Frederick William I burned with the desire to force Frederick to renounce the succession but thought better of it since the Imperial Diet of the Holy Roman Empire would disapprove. *How dare he challenge my authority!* thought Frederick William. *Not only that but his son's perversion would become widely known and it was an embarrassment to the Hohenzollern name! This has to be stopped! First he formed an attachment with one of my pages and now this, this infatuation with Katte. It has to end!*

Thus, the following day, Frederick William I forced his son to witness the decapitation of his lover, Hans. Frederick's anguish caused him to faint. Although pardoned, he was stripped of his military rank and forced to stay at Küstrin under strict and strenuous tutelage for his future role by members of the state and war departments. When she could safely get away, his mother visited him and his father allowed him to return briefly to attend his sister's wedding. Finally, he was allowed to return to Berlin permanently. However, the following year he was forced into an arranged marriage with Elisabeth Christine of Brunswick-Bevern. While it cast him into deep depression, he knew it was inevitable. But he had no intention of having children and was quite happy to let one of his younger brothers be his successor.

When the War of Polish Succession burst forth, Frederick led his Regiment in support of Prince Eugene of Savoy. His first evening was transformational; he couldn't help a grin from appearing. Prince Eugene was not only a consummate military hero but also had a preference for men!

* * *

After Louis XIV died, peace was preferred in order to recuperate financially, expand trade, or to protect a vulnerable hereditary throne. In France, the regency had ended and Cardinal Fleury, Louis XV's former tutor, was the major influence in terms of policy and he promoted peace as did Robert Walpole in Britain. Peace, that is, unless, something came up that would further weaken one of their adversaries. For France, this came to the fore in 1733 when Augustus II of Poland died. In England, Annibel and Eric Bennet, and Eric's friend, Adam, were discussing the news that they had just read in the *London Gazette*.

"Why didn't the others just stay out of it?" asked Annibel.

"Because Poland's only value is as an ally. If a Pole were in control, they might stay neutral or give aid to your enemy. The Sejm met and decided that the throne should be held by a Pole instead of a foreigner. However, their neighbors didn't agree," said Eric.

"Who were the leading contenders?"

"Basically there were three. Augustus II's son, Frederick Augustus II of Saxony, Stanislaw Leszczynski whom Charles XII of Sweden had put in to replace Augustus II during the Great Northern War, and Emmanuel of Portugal. France, backed by Spain, supported Stanislaw against Austria joined by Russia and Saxony."

"Why Russia?"

Adam answered for Eric, "Because Anne was married off to the Duke of Courland and he sided with Saxony. Britain and the Netherlands had the good sense to remain neutral. During the first year, several secret treaties were signed as everyone involved tried to leverage their support or forfeiture of some position for a better outcome for themselves. Now, here we are a year later, the fighting is over and Frederic Augustus II has taken the throne as Augustus III."

"Did anyone gain?" asked Annibel.

"To some extent France did because Stanislaw was given Lorraine which will fall to France when he dies. Plus, France and Austria had agreed on détente and might actually become allies when the next confrontation occurs. Charles VI of Austria's heir is Maria Theresa and while everyone has signed the Pragmatic Sanction where they have promised to recognize her as Queen, I doubt they will keep their word," Adam theorized.

"Once again," interjected Eric, "the real loser is Italy. The Duke of Lorraine gave that position up to become Duke of Tuscany, the Duke of Parma gave up Parma to become King of Naples and Sicily, and the Duke of Sardinia received additional territory in the western region of Milan. God only knows how the Italians feel about all these changes which only again proves Machiavelli was correct in saying Italy had to unify and develop its own standing army or it would always be at the mercy of foreign monarchs."

"What news in the dispatches from India?" Adam asked Eric.

"It doesn't portend well for the Moghuls. It seems to be imploding."

"What do you mean?"

"Well, it seems that Aurangazeb failed to keep to the tenets of his forefathers. The Marathas, under the devout Hindu, Shivaji, have long been a problem and it appears Persia is not helping."

"How so?" asked Adam.

"Nadir Shah seized the throne from the Safavids and then proceeded to extend his rule north into Kandahar and then Kabul two years later. This meant that he now controlled the Khyber Pass and entry into India."

"Did he follow up?"

"Yes, indeed. Aurangazeb's successor Mohammed Shah failed to defeat Nadir and so he took Delhi."

"Is his intention to stay and conquer more territory?"

"No, it appears looting the riches from Delhi including the Peacock Throne and the Koh-i-Nur diamond, satisfied his acquisitive instincts. I heard that the loot taken will allow him to suspend taxation of his own people for three years! It is a disaster for the Moghul Empire and internal divisions are only going to get worse."

"Sounds like the exploits of Timur three hundred years ago," commented Adam.

"Well, there is no question that we will have to make sure we support the winning side or France will usurp us in trade and influence in that region."

* * *

In South Carolina, a slave rebellion was about to take place. On September 9, 1739, a Sunday, most white families would rise and attend their local church service. A recent law, the Security Act, required all men to take their muskets with them. The probable reason for such was the growing uneasiness they felt over the disproportion of slaves to whites in the colony and the recent exposure of a planned slave revolt before it could be put into effect. Before dawn, on the Stono Bridge about twenty miles west of Charleston, a group of slaves had congregated around their leader, Jemmy.

"It's time. We either do it now or continue to suffer and I'm fed up. It's not fair and it's only going to get worse."

"But where will we go?" asked Jim.

"South, to Florida. The Spanish promise freedom to all who come."

"That's a mighty long way and we don't have muskets. You know they'll come after us."

"We'll take them from the shop in town."

The others were silent. The mood was fatalistic but energizing as well. These men had reached their limit and were far beyond docile subservience.

"Let's go."

Having stolen guns from the shop and killing the two clerks, they headed south on the dusty road, knowing that there was no turning back. Others joined them. Any whites they met were killed or fled. One who managed to get away was Lt. Gov. William Bull who raised the alarm. By now fifty to sixty blacks had reached the Edisto River, about ten miles from where they had begun. It was here that they would have to fight the whites who had organized and pursued them. By nightfall, it was over; half lay dead and those who had managed to escape were hunted down and executed. Fear of another such uprising led to even stricter laws.

Those left behind waited for news of the almost spontaneous uprising. One young slave, John, saw his chance. He snuck into the kitchen when the cook was in the garden and stole some food and a carving knife. Making sure he was not seen, he fled west through forests and fields, past the frontier into Cherokee territory. He had no idea how he would be received by the Indians but anything was better than spending the rest of his life as a slave.

Chapter 23

The Rise of Methodism

While the Enlightenment and the philosophes' literature grew over the decades, there were some in the Church of England who sought enlightenment of a different sort. They did not share the view that reason was more important than feeling. They felt that religion had lost the ability to warm the heart. Thus, several members of the established Church in England and in New England, developed a preaching style that challenged the staid and frankly dull weekly service. They also sought to reach those who were lapsed sinners who no longer attended any service.

In England, the Wesley brothers, John and Charles, as well as their friend, George Whitefield, held widening differences with the Anglican Church. At Oxford, they had formed a Holy Club that aimed at reinvigorating faith against the rising tide of reason. Their position held that feeling had an equally important role and should not be forsaken.

In 1736, John Wesley went to serve as a minister in Savannah, Georgia. The most lasting effect upon Wesley occurred on the voyage to America. During a frightful storm when the crew and passengers feared for their lives, a small group of Moravians calmly sang hymns. Such demonstration of faith was amazing. Over his two year stay, a controversy over denial of confirmation of a parishioner, Sophia Hopkey, that many felt stemmed from personal pique at her rejection of his advances, led to his dismissal. He returned to England depressed and unsure of his own faith. Listening to a sermon on one of the works of Martin Luther, he felt rejuvenated. Over the ensuing years, he developed a new method of reaching out, particularly to those who were disadvantaged and never went to church: preaching in an open field.

In 1738, George Whitefield followed Wesley to Savannah. He would return to England because of the need he saw in this poor colony, the need for an orphanage. Thus, he returned to raise funds for such a project. He reunited with the Wesley brothers even though he disagreed with them over certain doctrines such as predestination, which Whitefield accepted, and atonement, which he did not. Nevertheless, these Methodists as they came to be known, although disliked by traditional clergy, continued their work with the unconventional method of preaching in the open air. It was here that Whitefield, with incredible dramatic flair, awoke those who came to listen from their long apathy to religious teaching and experience.

Just as the first Awakening was developing in England, it was also growing in America. The first American to re-invigorate theology in New England was Jonathan Edwards. Over his years of training, he would engage in walks in nature, reveling in its beauty, simplicity, and perfection. *How could God create such magnificence and condemn those not of the elect to Hell? What a terrible doctrine. Nothing is predestined. All can win redemption if given a chance to really believe* he thought.

Edwards married the daughter of the President of Yale College, Sarah Pierpont, whose family tree on her mother's side went back to Thomas Hooker, a founding father of the Congregational Church in Connecticut. When Jonathan graduated from college, he assisted his grandfather, Solomon Stoddard, in Northampton, a large and wealthy congregation. Upon Stoddard's death, Edwards was appointed to take his place. His parishioners were awakened by the sincerity of his beliefs and the hope he instilled in their salvation. His sermons were published and read in America and Europe.

The Awakening continued to grow in America when Whitefield returned there in 1740. Having visited New England and New York City, Whitefield passed through Philadelphia where he again met Benjamin Franklin, a confirmed Deist. Having heard of Whitefield's desire to preach to raise funds for an orphanage in Georgia, the ever practical Franklin suggested building the orphanage in Philadelphia and bringing the children there so as not to waste money in sending materials to Georgia. However, Whitefield was adamant, thus, Franklin went to hear him preach, determined not to contribute a penny but to see if the crowds he drew were really noteworthy since some papers he had read suggested attendance at 25,000! Ridiculous! If you had seen Whitefield but had never heard him preach, you wouldn't believe it either. His stature was unimpressive and his eyes crossed in a very distracting way. When he came to the raised platform, a silence descended upon the crowd gathered. And then, when he spoke, it was mesmerizing. His enunciation and resonance were incredible. His voice clearly projected to the farthest reaches of the people raptly listening to his exhortations to believe, to feel, to experience the wrath and forgiveness of God.

"My word, that preacher was sumtin! He's sure right about one thing"

"Wa's that?"

"We're all part devils." The others laughed.

"He sure knows about fire and brimstone. My life isn't worth much; never has been, never will be, but I guess I could try harder."

The others paused as if to reflect and most wore a look of resigned agreement.

"I knew I'd end up in even worse times if I stayed in London so why not indenture. The ships were the same as they use for slaves. At least we didn't have to wear irons," someone else put in.

"Maybe for you but I was transported and we were kept chained."

"Whad's you do?"

"I lifted some food cause I was starving."

"Still many died of starvation if the trip took too long. This may be the land of plenty but only a few benefit. My master wanted to get as much out of my labor as he possibly could. Hell, slaves are better fed because they're property. I curse property. How can you get property? Only way is to live on the frontier and die fightin Injuns."

"It ain't right but what are we poor folk supposed to do. Can't change the law cause we don't have property.

"I dunno but that preacher seemed to care, at least about my soul."

"We're just the dregs at the bottom of the barrel."

When Franklin returned home, he recounted the experience to his wife, Deborah. "Incredible. All are dwarfed in his emotive capacity on stage. It was truly amazing. Even I was moved to contribute, and then listening to him, I decided to contribute more. Finally, when it was over, I emptied my pockets. It was an awakening of sensitivities and even skeptics, such as myself, were moved by his genuine belief in his message."

Whitefield and Franklin became close friends over the ensuing years based on mutual respect for the other. Although Whitefield never converted Franklin, he never gave up trying. Franklin became the publisher of his sermons and they kept up a steady correspondence after Whitefield returned to England. Among the qualities each admired most about the other were integrity and commitment to values.

Chapter 24

Fighting for That Which is Mine!

Two years after the Treaty of Vienna had been ratified, Charles VI of Austria died. Maria Theresa assumed the throne. Would other countries honor the Pragmatic Sanction? That was the question on everyone's mind. Many of the Austrian elite assumed her husband, Francis, would be the real ruler with Maria Theresa being merely the figurehead. This seemed to be her intention when she referred to him as co-ruler but this, along with his new title of King of Bohemia, was only to secure his election as Holy Roman Emperor, a role she could not fulfill. Once this was secured, it was quickly made clear that she was the absolute ruler of Austria.

Opposition arose within the Empire first from Bavaria whose army captured Prague in order to control Bohemia, and then from Prussia, which snatched Silesia. Although she would regain Bohemia with the help of Hungary, she had to concede Silesia to Frederick II. She silently vowed that one day she would get it back!

* * *

In Russia, internal tension had grown as to whom should rule. Jean Armand Lestocq had requested a private meeting with Elizabeth. The two were now seated in her study. Jean Armand quickly got to the point. "Now you must act!" he said. "For the third time, you have been unfairly passed over. Why? The Dolgorukovs thought they could use Anna as their pawn. But she and her German lover Biron had other ideas. She eliminated Russian oligarchs and replaced them with Germans. Then when she lay dying she chose Ivan VI, the two-month old son of Anna Leopoldovna, her sister. This is ridiculous. Russia needs a Tsar who will rule in the interests of Russians, not Germans. You are your father's daughter and must return us to the course he envisioned. The people will support you. The Preobrazhensky Regiment will follow you!" said Jean Armand Lestocq.

"So be it. We must move quickly," said Elizabeth.

Later Lestocq met with the French Ambassador to Russia, the Marquis de La Chétardie. When informed of Elizabeth's decision, he said, "Let the officers of the Imperial Guard know that there will be financial incentive for those who back Elizabeth."

Thus, on November 25, 1741, the Preobrazhensky Regiment marched on the Winter Palace and arrested the infant Ivan I, and his parents. Elizabeth became Empress of Russia. However, she had no intention of marrying as she was involved in a long-standing love affair with Alexis Razumovsky, a Ukrainian serf who had been bought to serve in the St. Petersburg choir. He had no political ambition and shared her love of music and the arts. However, she would need an heir and settled upon her sister's son, Peter Ulrich. She invited him to come live in St. Petersburg so that she could guide his instruction for when he assumed his duties as Tsar. M. Staehlin, had been hired as Peter's tutor and met with the Empress.

"May I speak freely, Your Highness?" asked Staehlin.

"Yes, it is necessary," said Elizabeth.

"Peter is very resistant to my attempts to educate him for the role as your successor. He seems to have been cruelly treated by his former tutor and acts of cruelty toward his pets are not uncommon."

"I am aware of his ignorance and dearth of social grace," said Elizabeth.

"Well, quite frankly, he seems to have no desire to become Emperor. His physical and emotional development seems to be arrested. He spends time playing with toys, especially his toy soldiers."

"Then we must find him a sensible wife and secure the line of succession as quickly as possible. If necessary, I will ensure that their child is my successor and choose a sensible regent," said Elizabeth.

"As you wish. Do you have anyone in mind?"

"I will think on the matter. Thank you."

Having dismissed Staehlin, Elizabeth pondered her choices. Having few allies among the Russian aristocracy who had favored Peter I's half-brother Ivan's descendants, she looked elsewhere. Her sister, Anne, Peter Ulrich's mother, had wed Charles Frederick, Duke of Holstein-Gottorp, who was also the nephew of Charles XII of Sweden. Long ago, Elizabeth was to have married Charles Frederick's cousin, Charles Augustus, but he had died before the nuptials could take place. *However, he had a sister, Joanna, who had married a much older man. What was his name? Ah, yes, Christian Augustus of Anhalt-Zerbst who served in the Prussian army and they lived in the town of Stettin. They had a daughter. What was her name? Ah, yes, Sophia. Hmmm.*

In Stettin, Joanna sat in the parlor with her face expressing her perpetual dissatisfaction with life. She had almost died after her first pregnancy and had never reconciled herself with the fact that her suffering was for a daughter, not a son. She wanted a son who would be in line for possible inheritances elsewhere and rescue her from this dreadful town on the Baltic. Daughters were useless! Years had passed and she had never forgiven Sophia for being a girl. A footman interrupted her thoughts and, with a slight bow, handed her a letter.

She opened it and a look of disbelief descended. Deliverance! The letter was from Empress Elizabeth inviting Joanna and her daughter to visit the Russian court. There was only one reason for such a request. Johanna was euphoric! At last, she would be the mother of the future Empress of Russia!

In the Winter Palace in St. Petersburg, Elizabeth was meeting with Prince Semyon Naryshkin. "I have invited Joanna and her daughter, Sophia, to visit. If our plans are to be successful, she will have to convert to the Russian Orthodox religion. Thus, I have specifically excluded her father, a devout Lutheran, from accompanying them. Semyon, you will meet them at Riga, provide them with a suitable wardrobe for appearing at court, and escort them to Moscow." Prince Naryshkin bowed and left to prepare for the trip to Riga.

Meanwhile, on their journey west to Riga, Joanna and Sophia visited the court of Frederick II in Berlin. Having had France and Austria allied against him in the war following Maria Theresa's ascension to the throne, he saw great benefit in keeping Russia neutral, if possible. Frederic welcomed them and insisted that they remain for dinner. He even seated Sophia at his own table in order to converse with her. Joanna was displeased at being placed at a table with less important ministers.

"Tell me, Sophia, you seem to be extremely well educated in French literature, are your parents inclined to favor the French?"

"Thank you, Your Highness. Not really. Actually, my dear tutor, Elizabeth Cardel, was a French Huguenot. She loved literature and music, especially opera, as do I. I shall miss her."

"Yes, when not forced to the call of arms, I, too, have found great solace in the arts. I subscribe to works by Voltaire and others. Music is a comfort to my soul and I am especially fond of the flute."

Later that evening, Frederick II did have a separate conversation with Johanna expressing the desire that she represent his interests in the Russian court.

"Vice-Chancellor Bestuzhev is, unfortunately, very anti-Prussian. You will find my Ambassador a helpful ally and I will see that you are generously rewarded."

In Riga, Joanna and Sophia met Prince Naryshkin and they were provided with an extensive wardrobe, at least extensive for Sophia who only had three dresses to her name although her mother had brought a large wardrobe of her own. And the sable furs that they were draped with kept them warm as the sledges carried them across the glistening snow to Moscow.

When all were congregated in the Winter Palace's ornate dining room, Elizabeth was overwhelmingly impressive in her gorgeous attire and bedecked with jewels. Peter had just turned sixteen and the contrast with his vibrant, attractive, vivacious aunt could not have been more striking. He was short and ugly with protruding eyes. Sophia couldn't have cared less. He was her escape from her mother's incessant domination and constant criticism.

The next morning, Elizabeth met with her Vice-Chancellor Bestuzhev. "Well, what do you think? Will she do?" asked Elizabeth.

"Actually, yes, I think you have made a wise choice. She seems genuine, was kind to Peter, and seems reasonably well educated. She even said her very first desire was to learn Russian. All in all, Peter and she should do quite well. However, I would not say the same for her mother. She only cares about herself and seemed to be very interested in the Ambassadors, La Chetardie and Mardefelt. I shall keep my eye on them."

"Do that. There is no question that they seem to favor Prussia. Frederick II now has Silesia and, I am sure, aspirations for more."

Bestuzhev's suppositions about a conspiracy between Joanna and the French and Prussian Ambassadors proved correct and Elizabeth ordered their recall. She allowed Joanna to remain for the betrothal and wedding ceremonies but she was then sent back to Stettin. Meanwhile, Sophia mastered the Russian language and under the tutelage of Simon Todorsky, she converted to the Russian Orthodox religion. Elizabeth insisted she change her name as it was associated with a relative she despised, and thus, Sophia became Catherine.

* * *

While Elizabeth was consolidating her rule in Russia, in China, Hongli became Emperor and adopted the era name Qianlong. His father, Yongzheng, had included Hongli in court discussions and he was well prepared to assume control. Under his long rule, China would continue to expand to include many non-Han people but over time relative peace descended and the arts flourished.

Chapter 25

Roles are not Always a Given

In Chelsea, Alice Bennet and her daughter, Annibel, were awaiting the arrival of Alice's husband and his guests from London: a fellow merchant, Richard Boddicott, his wife, and a young lady in his charge, Eliza Lucas. Shortly before dinner, the coach arrived and the Boddictotts and Eliza were welcomed as introductions were made. Then they all proceeded inside to dine. The two girls sat together on one side of the long table.

"Mr. Boddicott said you were at school, a Mrs. Pearson's boarding school. Where do your parents live?"

"In Antigua. My father has a plantation and is in the navy. Antigua is the home port of our Caribbean fleet."

"You must miss them very much. Does it feel strange to be so far from home?"

Eliza smiled. "Actually, England feels like home and that's how we all see it."

"What do you study at Mrs. Pearsons?"

"The usual plus basic business."

"Really? Why is that?"

"When I return next year, it will be up to me to help my father with the plantation especially when he is called away on duty. My mother is very frail and I am the eldest. We also have three plantations in South Carolina."

"My word, I don't understand. Why have more plantations so far away?"

"Most of the islands are flat and all the land goes to the sugar crop. But we need timber for making barrels to ship the molasses, and food, especially salted meat for ourselves and workers." Eliza looked upon the gardens surrounding the house, "You have such lovely gardens. I read Miller's *Gardeners Dictionary*. Botany has always been my love but I must help my parents; my family is very important to me." Annibel and Eliza became good friends and when Eliza returned to Antigua, they continued to correspond with each other.

In Antigua, events were moving inexorably toward war between England and Spain. The terms of the Treaty of Utrecht led smugglers to try to exceed the amount of goods England could supply to Spanish colonies and when caught, Spanish treatment was without mercy.

"Eliza, if, as I suspect, war comes, France will join Spain and the French will blockade our ports. I don't wish to disturb your poor mother, but I am making arrangements for us to move to one of my plantations in South Carolina. It will be safer and they are developing a new export crop, rice."

Thus, the Lucas family moved to one of their plantations that was located about fifteen miles from Charleston. Eliza was left in overall charge of her father's estates when Sir Robert Walpole declared war on Spain and George Lucas was recalled to active duty. Both the islands and the southern colonies in America were hurt by wars because their economies were so dependent on trade. Fortunately, Eliza's neighbors were very willing to help her adjust to her new circumstances. These included the Clelands, Pinckneys, and a widow, Mary Chardon. Charles Pinckney was a lawyer and taught Eliza the rudiments of preparing wills as her neighbors also included subsistence farmers. These less educated members of society often left writing a will until they were close to death and calling a lawyer from Charleston took too long. Eliza learned how to do it for them. The slaves on the Wampoo plantation also appreciated her teaching their children along with her sister Polly.

Being in charge allowed Eliza to indulge her love of botany. She began to search for other exportable crops. She had determined that indigo held the most promise. Her father encouraged her efforts and sent Nicholas Cromwell to guide her in the process of planting and harvesting indigo as well as how to construct vats to separate the dye from the husk.

"I don't understand it. This is the third year and we still can't produce indigo. It's so frustrating," said Eliza to her mulatto overseer Quash. "Why isn't this working?"

"Well, it may not be my place to say but I think Cromwell is sabotaging the project."

"What do you mean?"

"In the last harvest, he actually added too much lime to separate the dye from the husks and ruined the process. I don't think Mr. Cromwell wants you to succeed because he's from Monserrat which is a French colony and they want to keep their monopoly so that England has to continue to buy from them."

"But I can't give up. My father depends on me."

"I know Miss Eliza. Let me ask around and I'm sure we can find slaves here or in Antigua who know how to do it the right way," said Quash.

"Thank you, Quash, it's a good suggestion."

"You've been good to us. We really appreciate your educating the young'uns to read and write. We can do this Miss Eliza," said Quash in a confident voice.

Eliza's father did find a slave who knew how to grow and process indigo and sent him to help her. The next year's crop was successful and a sample of the dye was sent to England where it was judged to be of high quality and was sorely needed for the blue uniforms of the British navy.

Over the years, Eliza and Annibel Wentworth had continued to correspond. As Annibel finished a letter that she had just received, she smiled. Her friend had discouraged her father from contracting a marriage alliance until he had finally given up. Annibel knew that Eliza was very close to Frances and Charles Pinckney. Eliza was saddened by the unexpected death of Frances Pinckney. Now, Eliza was writing to tell her that she was marrying Charles. Annibel hoped that she would be happy. Her friend had had much responsibility thrust upon her and she must be somewhat relieved to have a partner. Annibel rose from her seat on the terrace and went inside to write a congratulatory note to her friend.

After dinner that evening, Eric and Adam were in the library, sitting before the crackling fire and sipping a glass of brandy. Adam looked at his friend who was staring intently at the flames as a strange expression flitted across Adam's face.

"What in the world are you thinking about?" asked Eric.

Before he could stop himself, Adam said, "Why doesn't she see me as a Man?"

"Who?" asked Eric, clearly perplexed.

"Your sister!" said Adam. Eric couldn't stop himself from laughing.

"It's not funny," muttered Adam.

"Oh yes it is. This from the man who enters a room and has all of the ladies swooning. It's priceless."

"I'm serious. Why does she totally ignore me?"

"But Adam, you know she doesn't. The three of us have been best friends for years. We go riding together, have great discussions, enjoy music and theater together."

"Stop. You know what I mean."

Hearing the frustration and sadness in his friend's voice, Eric realized that Adam was serious. "And if she did notice you in that way – what would your intention be?"

"Marriage of course. Love. Children. Happiness."

"Good grief. You really are smitten." Eric, seeing the frustration on his friend's face, smiled and said, "Adam, you know my mother was the same way. Mary Astell was her hero and she was a very independent minded lady. She and my father have raised Annibel to be equally independent. Could you do the same?"

"Of course! I don't want a subservient housekeeper. I want Annibel just as she is." The last was said on a wistful note. The two men were then joined by William Bennet and the conversation turned to diplomatic events. Eric felt that the least he could do was to ascertain whether there was any reason to hope that Annibel might return Adam's regard. The next day, he sought her out and, lacking his usual diplomacy, asked her if she had formed any attachment.

"Why Eric, what in the world prompted that question? Just because you seem enamored with Melisa Eldridge doesn't mean we all must enter such a state of infatuation." She smiled. "Thought I hadn't noticed?" she teased. He laughed, "Hopefully, no one else has as nothing is settled between us."

"I'll keep your secret," she said in a conspiratorial tone.

"But what of you. Have you formed any attachment?"

"No. Why should I? I'm too busy with my work and writing. I doubt there is a man who could match our father so why bother looking? Thank goodness Mom and Dad have never pressured me.

William Hogarth's latest work, *Marriage a-la-Mode*, is too true. Both parties end up in misery when they marry just for money."

"Well, what if there was such a person? Would you even notice him?"

"Of course, at least I think so."

The next afternoon, when the three were going for their usual ride, Eric excused himself, saying he had an important dispatch to write that really shouldn't be put off. "Enjoy your ride."

Adam and Annibel set off at a brisk pace that they both enjoyed and pulled up their horses on the crest of a hill. In the distance, they could see the Thames and sailing ships coming into or leaving the harbor. The sky was clear and a mild breeze ruffled the leaves of a nearby oak tree.

"Beautiful, isn't it; just like you," said Adam.

Annibel shot a glance at his profile, his gaze still focused on the far horizon. Suddenly, she felt her cheeks getting warm and realized she was actually blushing. Quickly she averted her gaze to the tranquil sea but she still felt funny inside. *This is weird* she thought. As she kept fixedly gazing on the horizon, Adam glanced over and was surprised to see her fading blush. *My word! Had he actually said it out loud? He smiled inwardly. Was it possible she might have feelings for him? Slow down. One step at a time,* he thought.

"Shall we return? We don't want to be late for dinner." Later that afternoon, he found the opportunity to accost Eric. "Did you say something to Annibel?"

Eric was no dummy. Something had happened on their ride. "Whatever do you mean?"

"You know exactly what I mean."

Eric grinned. "Not about you. Just general stuff."

Adam grinned as well. "Well, at least now the door seems open a crack."

"Time will tell. Honesty begets honesty. It's up to you now," said Eric.

Chapter 26

The Republic of Letters Expands

In 1742, in Paris, Denis Diderot met another young man, Jean Jacques Rousseau. The two had a great deal in common. Denis had left his home in Champagne and passed from a Jesuit college in Langres to one in Paris. However, he was not interested in pursuing a religious or legal career and therefore left college at which point his father disowned him. *Tant pis!* He was determined to become a writer!

Jean Jacques Rousseau, born in Switzerland, rejected an apprenticeship and left to travel into France where he was fortunate to come to the attention of Madame Louise de Warens. While living with her, he developed his musical skills and became a music teacher and copyist. As with many of the greatest minds, his intense desire to learn and his disciplined self-study led to erudition.

Diderot and Rousseau shared a similar casual life style, and became active participants in the Republic of Letters. They both married women of inferior station and continued to have affairs. Perhaps their motive in marrying was to have a housekeeper so that they wouldn't be bothered by the day-to-day chore of living. However, they differed in their attitude toward offspring. While Rousseau put his in a foundling hospital, Diderot had only one, a daughter, Angelique, named after his beloved sister and he would do anything for her happiness.

As an aspiring writer, Diderot was welcomed into the many salons aristocratic women held to further ideas through polite conversation. Needless to say, these salons were dominated by the males who would read extracts or discuss the topic of latest interest. Holding such lent more status to the woman running the salons and their primary role was to keep the conversation flowing and civil. Diderot had produced several works that included *Pensées Philosophiques* on the relationship between reason and feeling. Having casually disparaged the writing of novels, one of the female guests had challenged him to actually write one! *The Indiscreet Jewels* was published clandestinely and proved very lucrative. It was a lascivious tale about a Sultan who had a magical ring that he used to elicit sexual encounters. However, it was another work, *The Skeptic's Walk*, published in 1749, that would bring him to the attention of Voltaire.

Diderot and Rousseau became close friends of another man, Friedrich Melchior, Baron von Grimm. He was from Regensburg and had written a play that was reasonably well received but had come to Paris as tutor to the son of Count Schünborn. His French was impeccable, he played a cembalo, and, like his new friends, enjoyed music, the theater, and the salons. The three men often stopped at their favorite café before attending an event.

"I loath the censors! The Church has no right to prevent real knowledge from being available to all. Their Index of Forbidden Books is ludicrous. Myths are all they know!" said Diderot angrily.

Rousseau smiled sympathetically.

"Sorry. But I'm fed up. The Church officials have all the power but do they really do anything to actually improve the life of the peasant? Or the artisan? Or those orphaned or widowed and living in poverty? No. Just be patient and your suffering will soon be over and supposedly, your soul will rise. Stupid fools!"

"Which? Those who preach or those who believe?" asked Grimm good-naturedly.

"Both."

"And what are you?"

"Nothing. I'm a Deist."

"What's that?"

"I feel that God created and set the world in motion but it is up to us to determine the fullness of his creation. Newtonian science has given us the means to figure it all out."

"Do you believe in an afterlife?"

"I don't give it much thought. All I know is that I have been given life and I want to make the most of it and to help others do the same."

"Why do you think so many are religious?"

"A variety of reasons. If you're in the system, you have power and control not to mention a comfortable living, at least for the males." Diderot's thoughts flitted to his dear sister Angelique and the misery she had suffered when forced into a convent where she was literally worked to death.

"But why are there so many followers?"

"Because they feel powerless to effect change."

"I think some find comfort for their soul and enjoy the sense of community," said Grimm.

"Possibly but if they focused on the here and now instead of some after death reward, the monopoly of power of the landed aristocracy and certain merchants would not be as secure as it is."

"I disagree. Well, maybe not disagree but it seems to me it is man's frailty that makes him believe, the reward/punishment mentality of the people. Religious power is based on revealed wisdom of God. But, I agree with John Toland's *Christianity Not Mysterious*. God's intention can be understood through reason, not revelation."

"Well, the censors have made it very clear that *The Skeptic's Walk* will not see the light of day," said Diderot.

"That's unfortunate," said Grimm. "I found it a very interesting dialogue. But I'm afraid you're right. It reminded me of Galileo's work, *Dialogue Concerning the Two Chief World Systems* or *Dialogue* for short, which landed him under house arrest for the remaining years of his life. Remember his dialogue concerning the ideas of Copernicus and Ptolemy and a third undecided. I hope you have hidden the manuscript."

"Yes, I'm currently working on *Letter on the Blind* exploring the relationship between man's reason and knowledge acquired through what our five senses perceive."

Diderot did publish *The Skeptic's Walk* anonymously but other philosophes knew the real authorship and he was extremely flattered by a letter from the leading philosophe, Voltaire, commending it. However, eventually the censors knew the identity of the author as well and a *lettre de cachet* was issued. Thus, Diderot was confined to the dungeon at Vincennes Fortress. Rousseau visited him daily but such confinement was difficult. Fortunately, Voltaire's dear friend and collaborator Mme. du Châtelet was related to the governor of Vincennes and induced him to provide comfortable amenities to Diderot during his incarceration. Thus, he came out of the dungeon and roamed the halls, library, and gardens of Vincennes Castle. He was finally released four months later having agreed to disavow all of his written works just as Galileo had been forced to disavow his *Dialogue*.

"Good to have you back," said Andre le Bréton. "I have a job for you. I need a translation of Chambers' *Cyclopaedia, or Universal Dictionary of Arts and Sciences*. Would you be interested?"

"Certainly. I can begin immediately." Diderot returned home and skimmed through Chambers' work. He paused as his thoughts changed course. *Why translate a limited amount of information by an Englishman? Why not develop a French work that included the entirety of man's knowledge. To have all knowledge at one's fingertips would be fantastic!*

When Diderot again met with Le Bréton he suggested his idea and gave him a prospectus for the *Encyclopedie*.

"Interesting idea. A collaborative effort. Get various individuals to write on their areas of expertise. I'll run the idea by the censors. No use wasting our time if we are just going to have it banned. You'll need help. I'll talk to Jean d'Alembert. We'll sell by subscription. Many of our fellow philosophes might be interested in contributing."

Having received permission from the censors, Diderot brought Rousseau into the project to cover music and as word spread, many others joined as well. It was often the topic of conversation in the various salons, especially that of Mme. d'Epinay. It surprised no one that it sparked controversy but Diderot was convinced of its worth and would persevere on the project.

Meanwhile, Rousseau was also developing his writing skills. As a result of Diderot's encouragement, he entered a writing contest sponsored by the Academie de Dijon and won! *Discours sur les Sciences et les Arts* delineated the theme that he would develop in the ensuing years; that humans were basically good but corrupted by society's institutions.

* * *

At Mme. Tencin's salon, guests were gathering and there was an undercurrent of anticipation. Many of them had just read *De l'Esprit des Lois* and were eager to discuss it. Although published anonymously, many realized that one of the guests, Baron de Montesquieu, was the author.

"Tell me, M. Montesquieu, you have traveled to many different lands. Why focus on England, our major foe in war, in trade, in the fundamentals of philosophy?"

"Concepts are my guiding principal. In most countries, the king has the final word in setting policy. There is no check on his authority. Personal ambition can triumph over thoughtful policy."

"But that is the way it was ordained from the beginning," said M. Bonneuil.

"And what of the Church. They have authority over the souls of the people," said Abbé Reynal.

"That is true but the laws made apply to everyday people. Aren't they best equipped to make the laws that are to be obeyed?"

"You really think we should be guided by our illiterate peasants? Saints preserve us!" The others laughed in agreement.

"No but the Second Estate, of sword and robe, of literate gentlemen such as yourself might be included with some benefit."

"Tell me, a third power, the judiciary, what would they add to such a government? England, I believe, follows common law, placing an enormous power in the Lord Chancellor who is the only one who ultimately decides when precedent should be overturned."

"I agree. But if our Parlements only carry out the law imposed by the executive, we don't even have one person to defend rights which might be impinged upon."

"Well, one thing is for sure. The author was right to publish anonymously because the Church would never agree to forgoing their power. It will be banned," said M. Bonneuil.

M. Bonneuil was correct. *De l'Esprit des Lois* was banned and added to the Index of Prohibited Books. However, the work's reception in the German principalities, the Low Countries, and England was very positive. It would even reach the colonies in America where it was studied very carefully by those who subscribed to the philosophe's works.

Chapter 27

The Power of the Mind

Voltaire's relationship with Émilie du Châtelet led to collaborative efforts that proved fruitful. Her translation of Newton's *Principia Mathematica* from the Latin into French was progressing. She added her own commentary as she engaged in correspondence with other mathematicians and physicists including Leonhard Euler, Johann Bernouli and his student, Pierre Maupertuis. This resulted in publication of her *Institutions de Physique* in 1740. She also corresponded with King Frederick II who was invigorating the Academy of Sciences established by Liebniz in Berlin. He sent her various works by Leibniz and through studying his work, she developed the hypothesis on the conservation of total energy separate from momentum which contradicted Newton's assertion that energy and momentum were the same.

But in 1749, Émilie du Châtelet died. She had concluded her translation of Newton's *Principia*, which was published posthumously. The following year, Voltaire accepted an invitation from Frederick II to visit him in Prussia. Arriving at Sanssouci Palace in Potsdam, Voltaire was warmly welcomed as a fellow philosophe. During the ensuing days, Voltaire noted the marked difference between Frederick's court and that at Versailles. Although Frederick preferred the French language, he did not imitate the elaborate, ostentatious display of the French court. Life at Sanssouci was charming but simple and informal. The other guests and staff were all male.

"Come, let us sit outside. It's a glorious day. I read your work *"Elements de la Philosophie de Newton*. Did you ever meet him when you were in London?"

"Unfortunately, I did not. However, I did meet his half-sister and several of his followers."

"And was your story of Newton's apple on gravitational attraction true?"

Voltaire smiled. "*Bien sur*," he said. "His sister assured me it was so."

"Well, tread lightly with Maupertuis. My grandfather, Frederick I, made Liebniz President of the Royal Academy of Sciences. Now Maupertuis is helping revitalize it and he is now a strong supporter of Liebniz in his controversies with Newton. I believe your friend, Mme. Châtelet also felt several of his points were valid." Changing the subject, Frederick asked if Voltaire played an instrument.

"Alas, no but I greatly enjoy listening to great music. I understand one of Johann Sebastian Bach's sons works for you."

"Yes, Carl Philipp Emanuel, a charming man. Like all of the family, music runs in their veins," said Frederick II.

"Did you ever meet his father who recently passed away?"

"Yes, once, three years ago. Quite unlike his son. Johann Sebastian Bach was very stern, driven to compose, prolific in his output. *The Well-Tempered Clavier* was incredible. And, I have been told he had perfect pitch and insisted on tuning all of the instruments himself. He served Leipzig well. His work is very thought provoking, intellectual with incredible harmonic intensity. An amazing artist."

"Does such an artist have no equal?"

I remember he spoke of one, George Friederic Handel. Perhaps you heard his work when you were in England?"

"No, I confess, those to whom I was first introduced through Lord Bolingbroke were actually quite critical of his operas. Looking back, I suspect their response was probably rooted in jealousy. Addison had attempted an opera that was a terrible flop. However, it seems Handel was and continues to be highly respected and has moved from operas to oratorio. As you know, after composing *Saul* and then *Israel in Egypt*, his third, *The Messiah*, was very popular. It seemed to reflect the tone of the Wesley brothers new Methodism, awakening people from the lethargy of the Anglican Church."

"Frankly, I don't understand people's pre-occupation with religion. Toleration pays well in terms of our immigrants who contribute to the overall well-being of our life here in Prussia."

"That is a very enlightened view," said Voltaire smiling. "It is certainly one I would agree with, especially after all of my travails with censors."

"And yet you have eulogized Louis XIV in your history of the French Empire despite his expulsion of the Huguenots."

"Let us just say I focused more on how he brought France to its pinnacle of greatness; the leader in culture, etiquette, and fashion. Which is why everyone emulates France with perhaps the exception of England."

* * *

In Philadelphia, Benjamin Franklin was enjoying a very productive retirement. He was fascinated by electricity; whether it was static electricity caught in a jar or a jagged streak of lightening in the sky. Through experimentation and observation of the splintering heavens, he had learned certain characteristics of positive and negative attraction and that static electricity could be stored in a nonconductor such as the Leyden jar, popular with fellow amateur scientists, which he referred to as a condenser. He had also found that electricity could be drawn to a metal rod with a well-defined point and theorized that lightening in the sky could be drawn just as static electricity was and then it would pass through the rod into a container. Theoretically. Now, this, if true, would have a practical application. *Lightning strikes on church steeples, homes, ships on the sea,* he thought *causing death to bell ringers and igniting fires. But if the electric current could be caught and harmlessly buried in the earth? This had incredible potential.*

Later that evening, Ben wrote his friend, Peter Collinson, a London merchant, about his supposition that a pointed rod could capture and defuse lightning. Unbeknownst to Franklin, Collinson presented his ideas to the Royal Society and his detailed description in the letter was widely published. When it was translated into French, it came to the attention of the French King, Louis XV.

In the salon at Versailles, Louis had just finished reading the extracts on electricity. "*C'est incroyable*! Send for M. Buffon." When this gentleman entered, the king thrust the work at him. "Read it." Buffon, technically the king's head of the Jardin du Roi, had begun as a mathematician and become a member of the French Academie of Sciences. "Well, what do you think? Is it possible?"

"Intriguing. Why don't I test the concept with D'Alibard and de Loi. We will construct an experiment and let you know."

Thus, in the village of Marley on the outskirts of Paris, they brought a 40 foot insulated wire and as storm clouds formed, waited to see if anything happened. Suddenly, a jagged streak of lightening and thunderclap, sparks were seen and the electricity in the cloud, attracted by its point, traveled down and was buried in the earth. It was no longer just a theory; it actually worked! The king instructed his scientists to start production of such and said, "Please compliment M. Franklin of Philadelphia on his very useful discovery!" Because of the long time it took mail to cross the sea, Franklin was oblivious to the fame he had generated. However, he too wanted proof and had enlisted the aid of his son, William, to conduct his own experiment.

"Here, Will, hold the kite while I connect the wire and wet string. Wait, we need to attach something." He patted his pockets and drew out a metal key. Carefully, he tied it to the end of the wet string. "We're ready." The kite rose in the sky as the wind blew dark clouds across the heavens. But nothing happened. Maybe he was wrong. *Why wasn't it working* he thought. Just then, some of the strands of the wet string stiffened but before he could exclaim in glee, he cried out as his knuckle brushed the key and he quickly collected some of the charge in a Leyden jar. "By jove, it works. My word, think of it! The damage done by thunderstorms can be greatly reduced."

* * *

"*C'est fini*," said Diderot with a triumphant smile. "The first volume will go out to subscribers in a few weeks."

"It will be interesting to see how it is received, in the salons and elsewhere," said Rousseau. They both knew that elsewhere meant by the court censors.

"Just think of it! A compendium of all knowledge. The academies are so limited but we will cover science with opposing views, the arts and artisans. It is fascinating, compiling material on such diverse subjects but also collaborating with so many great minds. Le Breton tells me the subscription list is growing and I have received various offers to contribute to it."

As expected, the court took umbrage at some of the entries on the grounds of religious or natural law. But Diderot was determined. When the second volume was nearing completion, Diderot was visited one evening by a friend, Chrétien de Lamoignon Malesherbes.

"Denis. You're in trouble. The court has ordered that your work be seized before it is published. I presume to ensure censorship. You must hide it. As the local court official, I must send my men to collect it tomorrow. While I think your work is commendable, I must follow orders."

"Thank you, Chrétien, I appreciate your position. But my abode is modest. Where in the world can I hide the papers?"

"Give them to me. I'll bring them back when things cool down. Maybe I can get Mme. Pompadour to use her influence on the king to exert his influence on the censors to ease up."

The next morning, Malesherbes and his men arrived, did a thorough search and found nothing. Diderot had trouble suppressing a smile as they trudged out. True to his word, Malesherbes returned the completed manuscript and Diderot sent it to the publisher.

Chapter 28

Criminal Justice Reform

In London, at the Chief Magistrate's office, Henry Fielding was meeting with William Hogarth. The two had been friends for some time and had compatible views on the ills of society, corruption in government, and a commitment to effecting change. Fielding had begun his career by writing and had produced a very popular novel, *Tom Jones*, which covered moral behavior and choices in all spheres of society. Now he had accepted a more direct role in the criminal justice system when he became Chief Magistrate of London. Hogarth continued to produce widely circulated engravings that characterized moral choices and behaviors.

"William, thank you for coming. I could use your assistance. Please, have a seat. Some tea?" asked Fielding.

"It's good to see you, Henry. Thanks, a cup of tea would be nice. You should be proud of yourself. You've already begun to make substantial changes here in London and you're developing a reputation as one who is impartial, incorruptible, but with a sense of compassion as well," said Hogarth.

"Thank you, Will. Walpole's government was as corrupt as can be. His ability to speak German and insinuate himself into the king's good graces allowed him to rise to being considered the 'prime minister' but he used the position to enrich himself further. The whole system needs a great deal of work. Can you believe, some of the poor who are falsely accused of a crime and found innocent are then expected to pay the expense of their incarceration! If they cannot do so, they are remanded again to the Fleet Prison for debt. It's crazy. As we both know, Bambridge may be gone but it is still totally unfair to these poor souls. So I ignore it. I'm trying to reduce crime, not increase it."

"So, what do you have in mind? I will be happy to assist in any way I can."

"Well, your work is not only very popular but it is very influential as well because you allow people to visualize the consequences of their actions. *A Harlot's Progress, A Rake's Progress, Industry and Idleness*, all give the viewer a series of pictures as to the result of bad choices. What I want you to do, if you are willing, is to show the underlying cause for many crimes is inebriation. I doubt William III realized what he was starting when he introduced gin here in England. Distilled juniper berries are far more potent than beer and much cheaper. It's sold on every street corner and alleyway, not only men and women but children are consuming it as well. It causes people to do things that in their right state of mind they would never do. I want it licensed and to be expensive so that those who can afford it will drink it sparingly."

"I agree that it has become a problem but we both have to admit that for the rapidly increasing population in the inner city living in shacks and the filth created, the only water to drink is from the Thames and polluted with waste, both human and from the horses, dead animals, you name it. The rich can import spring water but the rest have no recourse. Although I will admit, it was better when there was just beer. Maybe tea could also be cheaper," said Hogarth.

"Well, I can't address all of the problems but I can do something about gin," said Fielding in a determined voice.

"Whatever happened to Christopher Wren's grand scheme after the fire of London?" asked Hogarth, "Didn't it include a sewer system and underground aqueducts to bring in fresh water? St. Paul's and other churches seem to be the only results. Anyway, with the rise in trade, any open spaces that were planned are now crowded with shanties, especially in the inner city by the docks."

"The wealthier citizens are gravitating to the periphery in Mayfair and rarely set foot in the inner city, unless, of course, there's a public hanging on Tyburn Hill. I don't understand the attraction but rich, poor, in between, come to witness the execution of the poor wretches. It's disgusting! I'm going to get executions made private. But I digress, sorry," said Fielding.

"Don't get discouraged. What you and your brother have started by organizing the Bow Street Runners is a great improvement. Only the rich would bother to report crimes and have action taken. The poor never bothered because no one did anything. If they made a stir they were turned upon and suffered the consequences. But your men are highly respected and, it will take time, but it will make a huge difference," said Hogarth.

"I hope so. It's especially important that we are now keeping records and the public has been very supportive thanks to the men who serve."

"So, down to business. You want engravings to help pass an act to curb gin?"

"Yes. The pen can only go so far but your satirical characterizations in the broadsides and dailies are seen by all. You are one of the few who can actually illustrate moral choices."

"I shall begin immediately."

Shortly thereafter, Hogarth produced two works, which were widely circulated. The first, *Beer Street*, depicted a scene where people were meeting in a convivial way and exhibiting decent comportment. The second, *Gin Alley*, showed the inebriation of all and the ill effects of such, centering on a small child falling to its death while the mother was oblivious and continued to enjoy her inebriated state. In 1751 the Gin Act was passed by Parliament and greatly reduced the access to gin by having it sold to licensed merchants who had to charge a much higher rate in order to buy the license.

Chapter 29

Tensions Rise in the Ohio Basin

Although there were many in the American colonies who remained poor, those that sought to become farmers and had the means to do so pushed further west. In western Pennsylvania, William Trent had established a trading base at the confluence of the Allegheny and Monongahela rivers, which came together and formed the Ohio River. His business thrived as all three rivers provided a transportation network for goods traded. Usually, trade involved furs in return for staple necessities. The French were not pleased with this intrusion into the Ohio River Basin, which they claimed as their territory.

As tension rose, Gov. Dinwiddie sent a representative to solicit Franklin's assistance in an arranged meeting with the leader of the Oneida, Scarouyady.

"Ben, we would like you to join Isaac Norris and Richard Peters in a delegation to meet with representatives of the Six Nations. They have asked for such a conference as well as more goods because of the incursion of French soldiers into the Ohio River Basin."

"Where are we to meet them?" asked Franklin.

"At Carlisle. We have arranged for you to have Conrad Weiser and Andrew Mantour meet you there to act as interpreters."

"Good, I would be happy to go," said Franklin.

"We will be sending several wagons with goods. Their primary spokes-person is Scarouyady, Chief of the Oneida."

Traveling on horseback, the three representatives soon outdistanced the wagons and in October 1753, they reached Carlisle and were met by Weiser and Mantour.

"You have made good time. The various tribal representatives should be here within a day or two. We have already had communication with Scarouyady. Evidently, the Governor of Virginia sent him notice of the French heading south to take possession of the Basin. The Indians have tried to deal with the French commander but he was adamant about his orders and his intentions to carry them out. He also told me that the French and their Indian allies have had confrontations, particularly with the Owendaets and most of their chiefs were killed," said Montour.

"That is why we have to present the gifts you bring as condolences before the conference can begin. Hopefully, the wagons will be here soon," said Weiser.

"Will Trent agrees with us that unrest will cause havoc unless we take steps now," added Montour.

Finally, the wagons arrived and the conference began, gifts were distributed as part of the condolences and then Scarouyady outlined the problems. What the Indians wanted were more guns and ammunition since those supplied by Virginia in the Treaty of Winchester were insufficient. According to their custom, they had sent three petitions to the French to withdraw, commanding the French to go north of Niagara. The French ignored these petitions. Now they were determined to fight. But Scarrooyady had other issues to discuss as well.

"In the future," said Scarouyady, "we would like you to limit traders to three trade centers so they can be protected. And, we need honest traders. The traders who have come only bring rum and flour. The rum ruins us. They cheat us. We need fair traders."

Having consulted with Franklin and Peters, Norris spoke. "We are happy to provide more but we must consult with our leaders. We think it wisest to leave the goods with one you trust, George Croghen, until he receives instructions from them."

"That is acceptable and we will consider you with continued affection if the trade is conducted as we suggest in the items we need and not just rum to besot our senses."

As Franklin and the others traveled back to Philadelphia, they discussed what had been said. Clearly the whiskey traders were undermining the Indians' ability to deal with the French. Ben thought of the Iroquois in western New York. It was a cohesive, well-organized tribe. And, although the Oneiga was part of the Iroquois Confederation, he had reservations about the Oneiga being as organized and effective. *What the colonies need is a militia that was unified. If the Iroquois can devise such a confederation, why couldn't we?*

When they met with the Governor, they stressed the ill effects of rum but also their doubts that the Six Nations could vanquish the French. Franklin put forth his idea of a militia to which all of the colonies contributed. He also expressed the need for the colonies to develop into a confederation. However, he remembered how hard it had been to get the Pennsylvania Legislature to set up a militia, which had led him to start a volunteer militia in Philadelphia. He also knew that the governor, representing the proprietor, Thomas Penn, would never support a tax for such purpose. The excuse given was the Quakers were non-violent. In reality, this Penn was trying to make as much money out of the colony as possible. Nevertheless, Franklin tried to see if the impending danger might convince him otherwise.

"In terms of defense, we need a colonial militia," he said.

"No Ben, you know I cannot approve such. However, I will consult with Lt. Gov. Dinwiddie in Virginia. Now, on another piece of business. You and William Hunter have been chosen to be Deputy Postmaster for the Colonies. Your friend, Collinson, seems to have been very helpful in securing this position." As the position came with a comfortable salary and the opportunity to travel to other colonies, Franklin was pleased. He had many ideas to improve its efficiency and was able to cut delivery time between New York and Philadelphia down to one day. In addition, he began the first home delivery system in Philadelphia for the convenience of the citizens.

As tensions with the French rose during the year, London also saw the need for colonies seeing to their own defense and called a conference in Albany in June 1754. There was even greater urgency for an organized plan when news came that Virginia had sent Major Washington and his militia to confront the French at Fort Duquesne. They had failed in their objective.

"My word, what happened? Who's Washington?" Franklin asked his friend James Parker.

"It seems that the French drove William Trent from his trading post and built themselves a fort. George Washington tried to talk them out of it but they refused so when he went back, it was with the idea of forcing them to withdraw. He built some sort of fortification, aptly called Fort Necessity, to act as a base to besiege the French but they were forced to surrender. The French destroyed his fort. Clearly, the Brits have to do something."

"Yes, but we could do more ourselves," said Franklin.

"Good luck in getting any of the other colonies to cooperate. I doubt it will happen."

"We must make it happen," said Franklin.

Later that evening he wrote an editorial and then drew a picture of a snake cut into 13 pieces, each labeled with the name of a colony. Underneath the sketch he wrote 'Join, or Die'. The cartoon and editorial urging the colonists to unite appeared in the *Pennsylvania Gazette*. He also wrote up an outline of his scheme to unite the colonies. He felt that American colonies should have representatives in the English Parliament. However, when the conference was concluded in Albany, no agreement was reached. The Indians from the Iroquois Confederation who attended were frankly scornful of the American colonies' weakness when compared with the French and Ben couldn't blame them. *We have missed a great opportunity to set aside our differences and unify. Things will only get worse,* he thought.

Britain also felt that the situation could not be resolved by the colonists and sent General Edward Braddock to Virginia to reassert British authority over the Ohio Basin. Governors Morris, Shirley, and De Lancey representing Pennsylvania, Massachusetts, and New York, were discussing their meeting with General Braddock in Virginia. Ben Franklin was also there at the request of the Pennsylvania Legislature.

"Gentlemen. We all know that after the failure of Washington to take Ft. Duquesne and the failure of the states to agree on a confederation of the colonies at Albany, we need the British army," said Gov. Morris. "The French are aggressively taking control of the Ohio Basin. We need to stop them."

"We agree with you, Robert, but frankly, Braddock is an obnoxious, conceited . . ." said Shirley but Morris held up his hand and said, "I know what you mean but right now, he is the one we have to deal with," said Morris.

"I think it is totally unfair that he refuses to do his job unless we supply him with horses and wagons. That's going to cost us a pretty penny!"

"I agree with you on his arrogance but if he succeeds, we benefit," said De Lancey. "And, thank you, Ben, for offering to handle the requisitioning of supplies. Do you really think you can get the provisions?"

"Yes, I think the farmers will contribute as long as they are well paid," said Franklin.

"Well, between you and me, the Proprietor's continued refusal to allow their estates to be taxed is disgusting."

Franklin was able to get the needed supplies but the farmers had insisted that he give his personal bond as they distrusted pledges from a general they did not know. General Braddock marched west, accompanied by George Washington. Washington had tried to get the general to work with the Indians of the Six Nations but nothing could dent Braddock's sense of superiority. "I see nothing that can obstruct my march to Niagara," he asserted. He would die as a result of his conceit. The British were ambushed before they even reached Ft. Duquesne. Washington, although wounded, and some of the others, were able to escape. The Indians of the Six Nations, seeing the weakness of British promises, withdrew their support. Many of the supplies of horses and wagons abandoned during the retreat were taken by the Indians. Ben Franklin faced a huge bill: 20,000 pounds! To recompense the farmers would ruin him financially. Fortunately, his friend, Gov. Shirley, who had assumed command of the British army after Braddock's death, ordered payment from army funds. The French and Indian War, as it was labeled in America, had begun.

Chapter 30

Portent of Evil?

"Please, Papa, can we go for our outing today. You promised we would go to the country," said Maria.

"Yes, my little one, but first we will go to early Mass as it is All Saints Day," said her father, King Joseph I of Portugal.

Maria couldn't help fidgeting during the service but soon the family and their attendants were on their way to Ajuda to enjoy the countryside. Suddenly, the earth began to tremble and the wagons halted. The horses' eyes rolled as they stamped their feet trying to escape their harness. An attendant ran to hold their heads. The royal family got out of the carriage. From their vantage point on a hill, Joseph and the others looked down upon the city. Before their very eyes, it seemed to crumble: houses, churches, museums, libraries, the royal palace: all cracked and fell apart. The water in the port seemed to be sucked out of the harbor. People were running or galloping away. Some had rushed toward the docks but stopped in frozen disbelief. A giant wall of water came back into the harbor and drowned all in its path. Two more huge waves would follow. Farther away from the coast, the collapse of the buildings had scattered the logs and embers from fireplaces. Tongues of fire grew to consume anything left in its path. The Royal family watched the horror unfold.

"Daddy, what's happening?" asked Maria in a trembling voice.

"It's an earthquake, little one."

"You mean like Pompei?"

"To some extent; that was an eruption of a mountain top. This one is an eruption beneath the earth or sea."

"Will it happen again?" she asked fearfully.

"I hope not." While he had no desire to add to his daughter's fear, Joseph resolved to never leave the hills of Ajuda and ordered tents and pavilions constructed to accommodate the royal family. As with the fire of London, Joseph would rebuild Lisbon and his Minister, Pompal, devised architecture that, hopefully, would not collapse should another earthquake occur.

* * *

Never before had anyone in Europe seen what most considered the wrath of God unfold in such a way. It was a disaster beyond their control. God had spoken because, as the English poet Alexander Pope wrote, 'What is, is right'. This infuriated Voltaire who wrote his own poem on the disaster that countered blind acceptance of a greater good even in such a catastrophe. Voltaire was a realist, a deist, and a skeptic. One must pursue critical reason, not fictions of the imagination, even if one admits, like Socrates, that one knew nothing. Dogma reiterated by Church and court officials was not a substitute for reason.

In Paris, Denis Diderot continued to work on the *Encyclopedie*. The constant harassment from the authorities was exhausting and although it was not very remunerative, the work he was doing was very fulfilling and he was determined to see the project through.

"Denis, may I come in?" asked Grimm.

"Of course. Dreadful news from Portugal. Imagine your whole life overturned or extinguished in mere moments. It's a disaster."

"A tragedy. I heard that Empress Elizabeth of Russia has offered funding for the rebuilding of Lisbon."

"Really! And the motive for such an act of generosity?"

"A kind heart, I suppose. Russia has nothing to gain. Elizabeth has had to take a hard resolve against Prussia but she has, on occasion, exhibited sensitivity. Remember, when she first took control, she forbade any execution as punishment. Just think of all the poor souls here who have suffered such a fate whose crimes are minor or not even real." Grimm paused, "However, I stopped by to discuss another matter. How would you feel about adding to your contribution to my *Correspondence*? You and Mme. Epinay have done a wonderful job reviewing plays but it would please me immensely if you would review the biennial art exhibitions at the Louvre."

"Certainly. I would be happy to do so."

"Good. Well, Voltaire is still trying to combat the Church in the La Barre case; it's insane. How can you behead a nineteen year old for mutilating a public crucifix. We need a rational legal system, not the tyrannical Catholic Church."

Chapter 31

The Enlightenment Expands

Moses Mendelssohn was born in Dessau. His father, Mendel, eked out a living as a scribe of Torah scrolls. Instead of the usual Jewish practice, Moses, in agreement with his father, chose to call himself Moses Mendelssohn instead of Moses ben Mendel, which was the usual practice. He was tutored by the local rabbi who recognized and encouraged the boy's intellectual potential. In 1743, when the rabbi moved to Berlin to teach in a Yeshivah, Moses followed him in order to expand his own studies. He mastered philosophy, mathematics, Latin, French, and English. He was fascinated by John Locke's *An Essay Concerning Human Understanding*. By 1750, he was fortunate to be hired by a wealthy silk-merchant, Isaac Bernhard, as the family tutor. Over the years, Bernhard brought him into the business as bookkeeper and then as partner. Moses never lost his thirst for knowledge. In 1754, he met Gotthold Lessing.

"Lessing, good of you to join us," said Aaron Gumperz. "I have a friend I want you to meet." Gumperz looked about the room until he saw Moses sitting by a table upon which lay a chessboard. Walking over, he said, "Moses, I would like you to meet a friend of mine, Gotthold Lessing." As Moses stood up, Lessing noted his affliction of a spinal curvature but focused on the quiet unassuming, intelligent face. "Moses, Gotthold is the author of the play, *Die Juden*. I think the two of you have much in common as representatives of the

German enlightened intelligentsia." Catching sight of a new arrival, he excused himself and left the two men.

"Do you play?" asked Moses, indicating the chessboard.

"Why, yes," said Lessing, " I would enjoy such."

'Tell me, if you would, what induced you to write your play? I'm assuming you are not yourself Jewish?" he asked.

"Reason. Traditions everywhere are being challenged, or will be in the future. For many, stereotypes are easier to accept than reality."

"Why do you think that is?"

"For those in power, to manipulate the people to their advantage in order to consolidate their authority. For those not in power, to derive a sense of superiority over another to escape being at the bottom of the social ladder."

"Interesting. I, too, see a growing spirit to use reason to establish truth. It seems to me that almost all of us have two worlds; the spiritual and what guides our ethical choices and what I would call the real world where we live, work, invent, form a system of government."

"Exactly. The Jews here are portrayed as low, miserable, and misguided. When intellectuals like Spinoza tried to expound on secular views, they were ostracized and excommunicated. Few know or acknowledge that Jews were in the forefront of learning and scholarship. Think of the Ummayyid Dynasty in Spain. Those Muslim rulers saw what a contribution Jews could make and welcomed them. Religion was a free choice; all prospered. But when the Muslim rulers were expelled from Spain, Ferdinand and Isabella demanded conversion. Thus, the dispersion of marranos in Western Europe and the development of the ghetto or isolated living arrangements, which alienated Jews from regular society. Those were Sephardic Jews. Here we have some Sephardic but far more Ashkenazi."

"Yes, the Ashkenazi are different because when Poland provided a safe haven by the Jagiellon dynasty, the system that evolved was not as inclusive. Thus, many continued to retain the traditional culture. However, Poland became dominated by the wealthy aristocratic families who lived in Warsaw instead of on their estates. They leased their lands to Jewish agents who collected rents from the peasants. But the owners kept raising the cost of the lease and so the Jews had to keep raising the rents. No wonder the Polish peasants went bezerk. But did they march into Warsaw and demand that the landowners stop raising their demands? No. They blamed the Jewish agents whom no one was willing to defend."

"Except you. Thank you. Such open mindedness is greatly appreciated," said Moses. Before moving one of the pieces on the chessboard, he looked up and smiled. "Now, let's see how open minded you really are. Check!" said Moses as he moved one of his chessmen. Lessing laughed.

"In all fairness, Jews themselves sometimes resist reason. Look at the self proclaimed Messiah Sabbatai Zevi. Despite his apostasy when the Sultan demanded that he convert to Islam or face death, he chose conversion. Jesus didn't claim to be the Messiah but he was willing to face the consequence of defending fairness," said Moses.

"Perhaps those at the bottom of the social hierarchy feel there is no
one who will stand up for them and, thus, the mystical constituent is appealing. A feeling of being accepted is important and when the religious hierarchy becomes aloof from the multitude, they turn to emotional feeling over learned rhetoric."

"I think that may be true. Look at the Methodists and so-called Great

Awakening or the growth of Hassidism in Jewish society here, piety over scholarship. The Hassidic practices are an emotional sharing of ecstasy experienced in feasting and singing as opposed to solemn prayer."

The two men became close friends for life. One of Lessing's later works, *Nathan the Wise*, reflected his admiration for Mendelssohn's mind and character. It would have influence persuading people to reevaluate the accepted givens of the past.

Chapter 32

Securing Alliances

When Elizabeth took control of Russia in 1741, she had been supported by the Preobrazhensky regiment. The dominant influence in foreign policy was Bestuzhev. The aristocrats were encouraged to be distracted by lavish court events modeled on Versailles. However, Elizabeth's one desire, to have Peter and Catherine produce an heir, was unfulfilled. Doctors were summoned but the cause was known to all; Peter had, as yet, no interest in sex, a case of arrested development. Years passed and Catherine had discreet affairs. Peter was tutored in sexual responsibilities. Finally, in 1754, Catherine became pregnant. A son was born. All accepted him as the legitimate heir. The baby was christened Paul and immediately taken away by Elizabeth to be raised as her own. Catherine was left with a husband who played with toy soldiers, an aching sense of loss over her son, and a depression she could only escape through reading. The works of the philosophes became her solace.

A new Ambassador from England arrived in St. Petersburg at the Winter Palace in 1755. The Major Domo greeted him, "Ambassador Williams, welcome to St. Petersburg. The Empress is feeling unwell but Peter and his wife, Catherine, will be pleased to see you. I'll show you to your rooms. Please join them in the Amber Room when you have rested."

Later that day, when they had gathered, Williams was remarking upon the unusual décor. The walls were an intricate mosaic of shiny, golden stones. "I've never seen anything like it. Do you mine the stones locally?"

"No, actually, it was a gift from Frederick William I of Prussia. His father, Frederick I had created it from the pebbles that are washed up on the Baltic coast. While they are hard like stones, they are lighter and their translucent glowing color makes them come alive. Mother is planning on moving it to the Catherine Palace this summer."

"It's very impressive. However, I was sent here to discuss Frederick II and his less than friendly attitude toward his neighbors, which my sovereign finds disturbing. King George would like to renew the treaty between our two countries for our mutual benefit. Of course, gold payments of the past would continue and hopefully peace be maintained." Williams was not yet aware that back in London George II had changed his mind and reached out to Frederick II. The two had signed a pact of non-aggression. If either was invaded by a third party, the other would remain neutral. News of that treaty infuriated France and Austria, long time foes now united in their hatred of Prussia. Notices were sent to Ambassador Williams by both George II and Frederick II, instructing him to assess who Russia would side with if war broke out. Listening to Peter's praise of Frederick II and his Prussian army, plus knowing that Catherine was of German heritage, he reassured them. He was mistaken. Catherine was not an admirer of Frederick, and, more importantly, neither was Empress Elizabeth. As a result, Russia joined the alliance with France and Austria against Frederick II following his invasion of Saxony. The Seven Years War, as it became known in Europe, had begun.

* * *

In London, William Pitt regarded those assembled with barely suppressed excitement. "Gentlemen, this is a great opportunity for the British Empire! While we will supply Frederick with funds and materials, it will allow us to focus on our primary rival France. While they are engaged fighting the Prussians, we will take the fight worldwide and drive them from North America and India! We must pressure the king to be aggressive."

"But what about Hanover?" asked Fox.

"We shall take precautionary measures. Frederick has agreed to stationing Hessian troops to protect our coast and Hanoverian troops will be under the Duke of Cumberland."

In Berlin, Frederick pondered his own strategy. *First we need to take Saxony, which is leaderless since their Elector, Augustus III, is also King of Poland and spends his time in Warsaw. Then we can add the Saxons to our own forces and take Bohemia, then Lusatia, then Moravia. If we have the Fortress at Olmütz, we can threaten Vienna and end the war on our terms* he thought. *And I will need more funds.*

Frederick was successful in his first move to take over Saxony. When he met with his finance minister in Berlin, he suggested a possible way to increase Prussia's finances. "Karl, now that we have control of Saxony, we can use the silver from their mines to help finance the war. However, it may not be enough and I have an idea to make it go further. Please send for Ephraim."

When Veitel-Heine Ephraim was announced, Frederick quickly got down to business. "I will give you the lease for the Mint if you agree to my proposal. We need more coin," said Frederick. "To make the silver go further, new coins will be of copper coated with silver. You have a network of friends, especially in Poland. Since Saxon Electors have controlled Poland, they have used coins minted in Saxony. Without its own mint, Poland would be the ideal place for the devalued coins. So, do you agree?"

"Certainly, Sire, I would be honored to assist you," said Ephraim.

"Thank you. I hope to bring the war to a speedy conclusion but it is always best to be prepared."

Once again, the power of finance triumphed. In the past, it had allowed certain Jews to become accepted in court society. Jews who had fled the massacres in Poland were not allowed to enter major German cities without permission. However, those who had helped finance and provide military supplies during the horrendous Thirty Years War became valuable assets to the crown, whether it was the Habsburg Emperor or German Electors. These 'court' Jews were allowed to build mansions within cities as were their families and friends. In addition, court Jews intermarried and became an elite group within Jewish society.

As Ephraim left, he thought, *I shall have to be careful. Rulers only treat us decently when they need us but when those needs are served, they abandon us. Remember the fate of Samuel Oppenheimer, Imperial War Purveyor for the Habsburgs. He made loans to the government on personal loans from a network of contacts. When the war against the Turks was over, he was never reimbursed. I must see my partner as soon as possible. If we can provide Frederick's needs, the rewards could be substantial. If they are forthcoming.*

But events did not transpire as Frederick had anticipated. The war did not end quickly. Both the Austrian and Russian armies were better prepared and organized than anticipated and, as a result, casualties were greater than expected. There were victories and defeats by both sides. Other German principalities joined to fight against the Prussians as did Sweden to the north. Prussia was surrounded and the outlook was grim.

France had tried to invade Hanover as their focus was also on their major rival, England. However, they were willing to leave if Hanover remained neutral. Once this was agreed to, George II sent Duke Ferdinand of Brunswick to replace Cumberland and reneged on the treaty. Brunswick and the Hanoverian forces drove the French south of the Rhine.

By 1758, Britain sent more funds to Frederick plus 9,000 British troops to supplement the Hanoverians. In France, the new chief minister, Duc de Choiseul, recognized that without Britain and Hanover, Prussia would be defeated. Frederick was facing stiff united opposition from the Austrians and Russians when disaster struck at the Battle of Künersdorf where he lost over half his army. And then the Austro-Russian army occupied Berlin. While he was able to retake Berlin, Frederick was staring at defeat. Yet, year after year, battle after battle, Frederick refused to end the war.

* * *

The construction of the impressive fortress of Louisburg on Cape Breton Island had been authorized by Louis XIV primarily to prevent the British navy having access to the St. Lawrence seaway. It soon became a thriving hub of the French fishing industry off the Grand Banks. French fishermen flocked to the site. Salted cod and barrels of cod-liver oil crossed the ocean every year. During the War of Austrian Succession on the continent, the British had seized the fortress, aided by the New England militias, but had to return it in the peace negotiations. Now, with war again breaking out in Europe, the British saw their chance to reclaim not only the fortress, but all of Canada. The successful attack would be led by Jeffery Amherst and assisted by James Wolfe. Pitt, now Prime Minister, then made

Amherst Commander-in-Chief with orders to attack the French from the south and Wolfe to take Quebec in the north.

In Quebec, above the sheer cliff on the St. Lawrence that protected the city from a direct sea attack, the French general, Montcalm, had split his army to protect land access from the north and south while a small number of his troops remained in the city. At the base of the cliff, Wolfe and his men gathered.

"Sir, Benny thinks he has found a way up the cliff."

"Really. Bring him over."

"Yes, Sir."

The scout, Benny, stood before Wolfe and proceeded to tell the general of his discovery.

"There's a ravine that I climbed, almost to the top."

"Is it possible for the men to climb?"

"Yes."

"What about cannon?"

"It would be difficult but if we have a couple of the fellows lift them with ropes, it's possible."

Wolfe pondered the choices. Could his men really go to the top? Time was running out. The leaves had already fallen. Soon the St. Lawrence would freeze. He estimated the cliff face was 175-185 feet high. It was worth a try.

The next evening, with painstaking care, over four thousand men with their rifles and two cannons crept up the path on the face of the cliff. Peeping over the edge, the scout saw one lonely guard keeping watch. With a rush, he took down the sentry and motioned for the rest to follow. Wolfe quickly got them organized into formation. When dawn lightened the eastern skies, General Montcalm was appalled at what he saw. The British on the Plains of Abraham! He couldn't believe his eyes. *Oh, my God,* he thought, *they came up the cliff.* He then saw the two cannons aimed at the city. *What if more cannons were hoisted up the cliff?* He couldn't afford to wait for reinforcements. Calling the forces available, he met the British on the Plains of Abraham. In less than half an hour, he had lost. Wolfe had been shot three times but lived to hear his men declare victory. Montcalm had also suffered wounds from which he died the following day.

While Wolfe took Quebec, Jeffery Amherst had moved against Ft. Ticonderoga on Lake Champlain while William Johnson took Niagara. By September, they had taken Montreal. French rule had ended in North America. While those in power breathed a sigh of relief to have the war over, not all Americans felt like celebrating. In Boston at Faneuil Hall, two friends on the fringe of the crowd, did not share in the celebration.

"What did we get? Nothing. American militia joined Amherst and Wolfe at Louisburg. Did we get any of the gold or silver stored in the Fortress? No. When they needed our militias to take Ft. Ticonderoga, they impressed our men, demanded quartering of their troops in our homes but never paid us."

"The only ones who will benefit are those living to the west who will push into the Ohio Basin. It just isn't fair. We do all this for the mother country but they did it for themselves, not us." Thus, the roots of separation would grow.

Chapter 33

Power in India

As in the American colonies, India was another sphere of interest between the French and English. The East India Company had established three presidencies to administer to the trade in Bombay, Madras, and Bengal. As Mugul authority waned, there had been rising conflict among the *nawabs* who controlled various sections of the country. Princes vied with each other, connived at getting rid of their opponents, and were only focused on their own wealth. During the turbulence, the British constructed a fort in Calcutta, one of three posts used for the extensive trade of the Company. In June 1756, the nawab, Siraj-ud-daulah, decided this was an assault on his authority and sent his huge army against the British in Calcutta. He quickly subdued the soldiers in the garrison and ordered them put in the military jail of Ft. William. This was a solid stone prison 18 feet square. There were only two small barred windows. Of the 64 forced into this 'black hole,' as it came to be known, only 21 would survive. One of the lucky survivors was John Holwell. Back in England, he was telling government officials of his ordeal.

"It was awful. We were forced in there in late afternoon. The monsoon was about to come so not only was it hotter then hell but humid as well. Sweat started to drip. We called for water but none was given to us. Most started to take off their clothes, their elbows and knees jabbing their neighbor as we were so tightly packed together. Those by the window got some air but they blocked it from the room and men began to faint from lack of air. They soon became corpses. Nobody cared because we were all focused on our own survival. When we were finally released the next morning, only a third had survived."

"Was this the nawab's intention?"

"I don't think so. He wanted to plunder our factories where trade goods are stored."

"Well, if it is any consolation for your suffering, Robert Clive and Admiral Watson have been ordered to retake Calcutta and force Siraj to agree to our control of the region."

In Calcutta, Robert Clive was meeting with William Watts, the East India Company's representative at Siraj's court.

"They are not happy with Siraj. He fears an attack by the Afghans in the north and the Marathas to the west. He should be afraid of those closer to home, in his own court. They don't like his aligning with the French since many of them have become wealthy from trade with us."

"Where is his army?"

"He has to keep it divided to ward off the threats I have mentioned from the Afghans or Marathas but a large contingent is at Plassey on the island of Cossimbazar."

"Is there anyone we could bribe to take his place?"

"Many but I would focus on Mir Jafar because he is the one already conspiring against Siraj. He's Siraj's paymaster."

Clive and Watts met with Mir Jafar and agreed to sign a treaty recognizing him as the nawab of Bengal. However, one of Mir Jafar's fellow conspirators, a merchant by the name of Omichund, demanded his share be increased or else he would tell Siraj of their intentions.

Clive, Watts, and Admiral Watson withdrew from the others. "Now what? If we agree, all the others will increase their demands. He's demanding three million rupees!" said Admiral Watson. Clive looked pensive.

"I have an idea, Admiral. Let's draw up two treaties. The one with terms we want on white paper that Mir Jafar, the Committee members, and you will sign. The other on red paper with Omichund's demand included. All will sign that one except for you, Sir. We'll have another forge your signature." Thus, the plot was put into action.

As the British troops descended upon Plassy, Siraj called upon the French for additional artillery. Fighting began on June 23rd. Clive decided to wait for night to fall and then they would attack. Suddenly, a rainstorm developed drenching all in its path. The British had thrown tarpaulins over their ammunition. When the rain ceased, the nawab's star general, Mir Madan Khan, led a cavalry charge assuming the British cannons would be useless as their powder would be drenched from the rain. He was stunned by the explosion of grape shot and died trying to retreat. Siraj fled and the British army officially recognized Mir Jafar as Nawab of Bengal. The British government, Clive and other officers, and the East India Company were well rewarded for the one-day Battle of Plassey. Robert Clive was one of the few who realized the long-term effect. He advised William Pitt to merge the three Presidencies of the Company in India into one administration under the British crown. His advice was ignored.

* * *

The Seven Years War ended with the status quo restored. Frederick had been saved from defeat by the withdrawal of Russian forces. In Russia, Elizabeth had died and Peter became Emperor. His admiration for all things Prussian led him to immediately end

Russia's involvement in the conflict. However, while fighting had ended against external foes, internal turmoil seethed under the new Tsar, Peter III. He had alienated many segments in the Church, government, and most importantly, the military. In addition, he had taken a mistress, Elizabeth Vorontsova, whose sister, Catherine Dashkova, had become a close confident of Peter's wife, Catherine. It was she who warned Catherine that Peter was planning to divorce her and make Elizabeth his wife. Count Nikita Panin, who had replaced Bestuzhev as Vice-Chancellor, had also heard such rumors.

"Empress, we cannot continue in this way. Peter is unfit to rule. He will make Russia a pawn of Prussia. Church officials are outraged at his secularization of Church property and fear he is, in secret, a Protestant. He has offended our military by making the Holstein Cuirassir Regiment supreme. The Preobrazhensky and Semyonovsky regiments have always been the elite and despise him."

"I know. The Orlov brothers are angry about his changes and lack of gratitude for their loyal service. What do you advise?"

"Peter must be forced to abdicate and your son, Paul, will be named Tsar and you will be Regent. The people will accept it. They dislike and do not respect your husband but have always seen you as a true Russian. You sat by Empress Elizabeth's coffin for hours to pay homage while he was off celebrating with his mistress."

"Would foreign powers accept it?"

"Frederick II would have the most to lose but he lost over half his officer corps and might acquiesce if we can make sure that England puts pressure upon him to do so."

"Very well. I will contact Stanislaw Poniatowski. Perhaps we could suggest a trade. We would support his bid for the Polish crown in exchange for him using his influence with the British Ambassador Charles Williams. He also has some influence in other courts."

Thus, a coup d'état was planned and came to fruition in June. Peter had gone to Oranienbaum to drill his Prussian soldiers, his favorite pastime. A manifesto then appeared in Moscow that Peter had abdicated. The Preobrazhensky and Semyonovsky regiments swore allegiance to Catherine. The Archbishop of Novgorod proclaimed her Empress and Paul was her designated heir. Vice Chancellor Panin accepted her elevation as ruler as opposed to regent.

"We must seize Peter," said Alexis Orlov."

"Yes, I will lead the Preobrazhensky myself," said Catherine.

Over 14,000 soldiers, with Catherine dressed in uniform at its head, descended on Peterhof. Peter fled but knew he had lost. He offered to abdicate if he and his mistress were allowed to go to Holstein. Catherine agreed and Peter was escorted back to Peterhof where he signed a letter abdicating the Russian throne. He was then transferred to Ropsha under guard. Catherine and the Orlovs discussed whether or not to let him leave the country.

"Catherine, you can't just let him go," said Alexi.

"I know. I need time to think this through carefully."

Catherine returned to St. Petersburg. Alexi and his brothers knew what had to be done. Alexi and the other guards invited their prisoner to dine with them. His valet was told he need not accompany his master. According to the letter that Alexi subsequently sent Catherine, they had dined with Peter, a fight ensued, and Peter had 'accidently' died. He assured her that was not their intention, and begged her to have mercy on those involved. Catherine was merciful. However, she was well aware that she needed a positive image in Europe and the death of Peter might fuel anger. She also knew that the philosophes had become very influential in forming public opinion in aristocratic circles. She had learned through correspondence with Mme. Geoffrin that Denis Diderot, in financial difficulties, was going to sell his library. Thus, she not only bought it for 15,000 francs but he was to remain its caretaker at a salary of 1,000 francs yearly! Needless to say, the salons were glowing in their praise and support for her taking control of Russia.

Chapter 34

Influence of the Salons

Back in Chelsea, England, Annibel, Eric, and Adam had been discussing the war on the continent. They had just finished dinner and had settled into the library.

"Oh, I almost forgot. Be right back," said Eric as he dashed out of the room. He soon returned holding a long rectangular package. "I brought you a present, dear sister."

"What is it?" asked Annibel excitedly as she took the package and ripped off the paper. "What is it?" she repeated in a bemused voice.

Eric laughed. "It's an umbrella. Like a parasol only this one you can use in the rain. I found it in a little shop on Rue Saint-Honoré . Ladies have used parasols in a decorative way but, it turns out, in warmer climates, they had a more practical application. They were often made of soft leather and used to ward off the sun. In Paris, Jean Marius developed a waxed toille parasol and then a French scientist, Navarre, added a longer handle and devised a mechanism to easily open it. Press the button and push upward."

"I love it! Thank you, brother. No more getting drenched when it rains. Now,

to return to the conversation we started at dinner, what saved Frederick II?" asked Annibel.

"Empress Elizabeth died. She had designated Peter to succeed her and he idolized Frederick. Not only did he withdraw from the alliance with Austria and France but he sent a corps of his own troops to serve Frederick."

"So is it over?"

"A stalemate. Hopefully, all parties will see the sense of ending hostilities."

"Now that Bute has replaced Pitt, will there be peace elsewhere?"

"Yes. Our biggest win is in North America. The French have been forced to relinquish all their holdings. Spain has the region west of the Mississippi and has given up its holdings in Florida."

"And in India?"

"The same. Their navy was no match for ours on the high seas and, thanks to Clive, we now control Bengal."

Just then, a maid brought out a pitcher of lemonade and glasses for their refreshment. After they had thanked her, the conversation resumed.

"Now that you are stationed in Paris, Eric, have you visited any of the salons?" asked Adam.

"Yes, it's a very pleasant way to spend the afternoon. The food and drink provided are delicious, and the guests eclectic. It is very similar to the coffeehouses here. Only here, like-minded men seem to gravitate to each other. And there are no women. However, most salons have at least a few women who keep the conversation less raucous and confrontational."

"What makes a salon successful?" asked Annibel.

"For centuries, my dear, the only voices to be heard were those of birth and riches. Whether in the First Estate, the Church, or the Second Estate, the nobility. The Third Estate was voiceless."

"So why are the salons different?

"Because entry is offered to those of talent, regardless of their birth or wealth. Their ideas, expressed through literary works that are increasing in an incredible way, allow them access."

"That would certainly explain why men of letters would come, but what is the motive of the women who run the salons?"

"That depends. For some, it is a form of education, denied to most women in the formal institutions, for others who are educated, it is a way to interact as equals."

"Do you have an example of such? It seems so rare."

"Probably the best example would be Mme. du Châtelet, a brilliant woman whose father was broad minded enough to see to her education. From what I have heard, she and Voltaire had a salon before she died. She published her work under her own name. Participants read the works to be presented and then broaden their minds through the ensuing discussion. Intellectually, even if one is wearing a dress, one can be appreciated by some males. Of course, there are other women who do it to augment their own prestige by playing hostess to important men. Some still favor the upper class. I doubt Mme. Deffand would put up with those I enjoy. It is only because of her adoration of M. d'Alembert that she tolerates the philosophes, with of course the exception of Voltaire whose reputation is so great it would be foolish not to include him should he ever return from Ferney. However, she now is willing to include any of the philosophes because of her competitive drive with Mme. Geoffrin. And, I must admit, Mme. Deffand has redeeming features. She has taken Jeanne de Lespinasses in as companion. That young woman, her niece, was illegitimate, impoverished, and consigned to a convent but Deffand recognized her incredible mind and has brought her into her home."

"What of Geoffrin?"

"She provides for all and was clever in moving her salons to the afternoon. Plus, she is very generous with gifts and patronage. But overall, you can't generalize. They provide the forum for discussions which we all enjoy."

"Are there any other notable women?"

"The woman with the most real influence is the King's mistress, Mme. Pompadour. She convinced the King of the wisdom of developing the manufacturing of china in Sèvres as well as better training for the military at Petit Trianon. Perhaps most importantly for the philosophes, she supported their work and defended them against attacks from the Church. Louis is truly devoted to her. And, she is pragmatic, a realist."

"I understand that Duc de Richelieu would not have agreed with your praise," said Adam.

"Yes, that is true. But why? Because Mme. Pompadour is a commoner."

"But I thought she is a marquise, with her own estate and coat-of-arms."

"Bought and paid for by the king."

"How does the Queen feel about her?"

"Actually, the Queen likes her. Pompadour is the only one of Louis' mistresses that treats her with respect, and even friendship."

"And what of Baron d'Holbach's salon. Is that considered the most important one?"

"He has birth, wealth, and talent; provides sumptuous meals and seems to be very generous to those who have only talent such as Diderot and Rousseau. I'm sure the discussions are quite animated in the all male atmosphere. And yet, the salons of females remain popular, possibly because the individuals attending have to be more circumspect and, thus, the goal is to explore ideas, not just to win an argument."

"Do women elsewhere hold salons?"

"Certainly not as many as in Paris but in cities like Vienna and Berlin they are emerging. And those in positions of power, such as Empress Elizabeth of Russia and many princes in the various German states subscribe to Grimm's *Correspondance Litteraire Philosophiqu et critique*."

"Who is Grimm?"

"He came to France as tutor to Count Schönborn's son and remained. He was part of the inner circle of Diderot, Rousseau, and Mme. d'Epinay. Since then, unlike d'Holbach who became a naturalized French citizen, Grimm did not and, thus, can distribute his two letters a month, which are printed in Zweibrücken in the Palatinate to evade French censorship. Plus, I have heard that they come with strict instructions not to make a copy."

"And what does he include in his correspondence?"

"A variety of topics: artistic, literary, social, and even political and religious critiques."

Chapter 35

Franklin Goes to England

During the Seven Years War against the French on the continent, referred to as the French and Indian War in America, Benjamin Franklin had foreseen that the issue of the Proprietors refusal to pay taxes along with the rest of the population was serious and needed to be addressed. The Proprietors' 5,000 pound voluntary contribution to silence their detractors would not silence him. An expansion and provisioning of a militia was essential. He had prepared a militia bill for the Pennsylvania legislature that was to be voluntary and allowed election of officers. He then set out as part of the militia to build a line of stockades on the frontier. On his return, he was elected colonel. Governor Morris and Thomas Penn were infuriated at his continued popularity.

"Now that England has declared war, we must be better prepared. Fortunately, attention is focused on the north. However, we too must be vigilant and contribute," said Joseph Galloway.

"I agree. The Penns want all of the rewards without any of the burdens. They do not honor their father's vision. They live in England and appoint Governors who see to their interests, not ours."

"Remember how they cheated the Delaware Indians in determining land allocution. They're a disgrace to their name."

"What we need is to deal with them directly. That is why we want you, Ben, to go to England."

"Well, I would be happy to do so. Might I suggest also that the Assembly offer to pay the new governor a generous salary and he might be more amenable to our wishes?"

"Do you know something we don't?"

"Perhaps. But I think the direct approach is also necessary. It will allow me to assess the decision makers and separate friend from foe."

In January, Franklin arrived in London and found lodgings with a Mrs. Stevenson on Craven Street. He made contact with his good friend Collinson who introduced him to John Pringle, a Scot, who was a professor of moral philosophy and who would later become the royal physician. Franklin was very impressed with Pringle when he learned of one of his humanitarian efforts. Back in 1743, during the War of Austrian Succession, Pringle had facilitated an agreement with the French commander in Flanders, Marshal de Noailles, to protect those wounded. Both sides agreed that they would be taken to a separate area, which was off limits to combatants.

Franklin was also introduced to William Strahan, publisher of the *London Chronicle*. They had actually been in correspondence for many years and would become close friends. Franklin was somewhat surprised at the warm reception from those he met as most of his friends in the Junto in Philadelphia had taken his scientific work on electricity in stride. Here he found it opened doors. He was welcomed by the Royal Society as well as other intellectuals, writers, and professionals. There were many coffee houses in the area and discussions were stimulating. But he was not welcomed by the Penns or their in-law, Lord Grenville, a member of the Privy Council. When Franklin's powers of persuading them to allow the Assembly to make decisions failed, he turned to the weapon he had used in the past, his pen. Strahan was happy to publish his articles in *The Chronicle*. He exposed their duplicity in dealing with the Indians and their forcing Governor Denny to resign when he became more responsive to the Assembly's wishes over those of the Proprietors.

While in England, Franklin spent time visiting Edinburgh in Scotland where he came to know David Hume and Adam Smith. They engaged in many discussions on human morality, defining the philosophes ideal, happiness, and the benefits of free trade. For Franklin, life in England was stimulating. He was supportive of England regulating trade and felt it benefitted the colonies to be part of the Empire. But he was adamant about the colonies right to make their own laws.

* * *

In many parts of the world as the end of the year drew close, many gazed at the sky. The Palmers, in Chelsea, and members of their extended family were there to celebrate Christmas. Annibel was watching her husband who stood at one window looking up at the sky. Walking over to stand by his side, Annibel said, "This seems to be your nightly vigil recently. Since when have you become a stargazer?" she asked with a smile.

Adam turned and laughed, "Ever since I was at Oxford, I've always wondered if Edmond Halley's prediction would come true. His work, *Synopsis Astronomike Cometicae* hypothesized that the same comet returned every 75 years or so. The last sighting was in 1682. So, if he was right, it should soon appear again."

He turned his gaze from the starry heavens. "Have I told you how beautiful you are?"

Unbeknown to the Palmers, the following evening Halley's long awaited comet was seen by the astronomer Johann Palitzsch.

Soon it could be seen by the naked eye and the Palmers were able to view it together.

* * *

On the Montmorency Estate north of Paris, Jean-Jacques Rousseau led a quiet existence of contemplation and writing. The swings in his mood had caused rifts with many of his acquaintances in Paris stemming from his growing condemnation of the chatter in the salons.

In Paris, everyone was discussing the fruits of Rousseau's contemplation. The first work to be published was *Julie, or the New Heloise*.

"Well, perhaps Jean-Jacques has exorcized one of the demons of his torment," said Diderot.

"Ah, you think it is to make Sophie d'Houdetot's rejection of him more palatable?" asked Louise d'Epinay.

"Unrequited love, here illuminated in great detail, is the fate of many women. Most are married off for convenience, as we all know. How many of them yearn for overwhelming devotion, for a man in their life who expresses such adoration. Such romantic novels will always find readers."

"It is certainly popular," said Denis.

"I'm somewhat perplexed by the allusion to Heloise. She was supposedly extremely learned for her time and, if I remember correctly, although she secretly married Abelard, she wrote in later letters that she had not wanted to do so as she preferred freedom to chains," said Frederic Melchior."

"Sophie d'Houdetot preferred her lover, Saint-Lambert."

"Well, the next piece we see from Rousseau will be controversial. It is an expansion of the essay he did for the *Encyclopedie* on inequality and political economy," said Denis.

"Speaking of the *Encyclopedie*, how are things progressing? Is it true that d'Alembert has withdrawn from the project?"

"Yes, he, Turgot, and others don't want to deal with the constant harassment after it was suppressed by the authorities. It's pathetic how those in privileged positions only use their power to improve their hold, ignoring the plight of the common people. It's exhausting but I find enjoyment in visiting and learning from tradesmen. It seems impossible to find rulers who solve problems and improve the lives of all the people."

"Perhaps we should all take heart in the Turk's message to Candide, to cultivate our own gardens."

"Voltaire certainly castigates optimism but if we only focus on achieving our own happiness, that seems cowardly. We don't live in isolated states of nature but are part of society as a whole."

"But if you see happiness as pursuing the truth and acting with integrity, doesn't everyone benefit?"

"Well, thanks to Empress Catherine, I can do both," said Denis. "She even said I could publish the *Encyclopedia* in Riga. How do you think she will do, Frederick?"

Melchoir considered the question. "I suspect quite well. She may have been born a German but she portrays herself and probably is by this time, thoroughly Russian. And in relation to what we were just discussing, she, like Maria Theresa in Austria, are indeed despots in the scope of their authority but hopefully, she will be an enlightened despot. Thus, work produced by the philosophes will have influence."

* * *

When Benjamin Franklin returned to America, he traveled through the colonies as Deputy Postmaster. He and Deborah had decided to build their own home on Market Street. The new Governor of Pennsylvania was John Penn, nephew of Thomas Penn. Although the war against the French and Indians was technically over, the Indians west of the Appalachians were angry at continuing colonial incursions into their lands. Pontiac and the Ottawa joined other tribes and rebelled against these incursions. The rebellion was put down with the help of deliberately infecting the Indians with small pox through blankets distributed by the trader, William Trent. Resentment rose by those exposed to this constant threat of frontier warfare and once again they marched to Philadelphia to demand protection. The Paxton Boys as they were called, brought to the fore the need for a permanent militia. It was, for Franklin, a stark example of the harm that was done by the Proprietor's refusal to be taxed to support a real military. The Paxton Boys were indiscriminate in their slaughter of peaceful Indians some of whom had even converted to the Christian faith. Franklin wrote a pamphlet that referred to the participants of such vengeful murders as barbarians. He was part of the delegation that met with the leaders of the mob and helped restore order. However, Franklin was appalled that Gov. Penn had no intention of punishing anyone for the atrocities committed. Franklin became determined to make Pennsylvania a crown colony. The Proprietorship had to end. Although even some of his friends were wary of such a move, he was able to get the Pennsylvania legislature to vote yes in a petition to the king to revoke the Proprietorship. And, they also voted for Franklin to return to England as their advocate.

Chapter 36

The Expense of War

In 1765, the Privy Council met to discuss England's financial situation. Prime Minister Grenville spoke, "In the last eight years, our debt has almost doubled! Since we have added Canada to our vast empire, we have two concerns: first, paying off the costs of the war and secondly, having a better administration and, thus, control of the colonies. In order to prevent another Indian war, we should establish a line of demarcation along the ridge of the Allegheny Mountains. We must also stop the colonial practice of issuing paper money. Might I also suggest we place a duty on sugar, and, we must stop the perfidious colonial smugglers." George III followed Grenville's advice. The Sugar Act and Currency Act were passed. England established vice-admiralty courts to try smugglers.

For most colonists, the peace was welcomed. In Massachusetts, the Chief Justice dealing with the implementation of these laws was Thomas Hutchinson, who was not really equipped to deal with such, nor did he represent the mass of residents. John Otis, a lawyer of repute, felt the position should have gone to his father. Thus, when the case on whether or not the government had the right to order writs of assistance came to court, he rose in strong defense of the merchants who opposed such searches of their warehouses and ships. Later, one of the observers in court that day, John Adams, recounted the scene.

"The man is incredible. He used the words of the famous English jurist, Coke, saying that the writs violated the English Constitution."

"I liked the part where he said that 'Everyman lived in a state of nature, that no one could challenge the right to his life, liberty, and property; that a man's house is his castle.' The passion of his oratory was incredible."

"Well, I liked how he labeled the writs as a destructive and arbitrary use of power, likened it to its costing one king his head and another his crown."

Hutchinson delayed action and Otis won election to the Massachusetts House of Representatives. However, those who knew him well were also aware that he could become extreme and erratic. Samuel Adams, John's cousin, led the opposition to England's increasing control. Otis drew up the demand for repeal based on the premise that there could be no taxation without representation in Parliament. Gov. Bernard shut down the session because he feared Otis would follow through on his threat to circulate his appeal in other colonies. He was too late. It had already gone out.

In London, George III failed to see the damage Grenville perpetrated, and had approved the Stamp Act. The Americans were incensed.

"How dare they! They have no right!"

"What in the world are you talking about?"

"Parliament has ordered a Stamp Tax."

"What does the Stamp Tax mean?"

"That every single document: wills, deeds, newspapers, pamphlets, almanacs, diplomas, even a deck of cards, needs a stamp to be legal. And, to get the stamp, you have to pay."

"You're joking. They can't do that. Are they crazy?"

"This is insane. We must do something."

When the Stamp Act had passed in Parliament, only one member had objected, Col. Isaac Barré. A copy of his speech opposing it was sent and circulated in the colonies.

"Listen to this. He is ridiculing the idea that we are indebted to England. He should know as many of us served with him. He's warning Parliament that their actions will cause 'the blood of those sons of liberty to recoil within them.' A toast to Barré!"

Reading this, Samuel Adams thought, *That's us. The Sons of Liberty. The Sons of Liberty will not accept this.* Adams and his supporters were determined to make execution of the Stamp Act impossible. Hutchinson had appointed Andrew Oliver as tax collector. The first expression of resistance was the hanging of Oliver in effigy from an elm tree on High Street along with other symbols of the despots in England. A crowd gathered as Samuel Adams watched in satisfaction.

Oliver told Sheriff Greenleaf to remove it immediately. But, the sheriff soon returned. "It's too dangerous. Frankly, you and your family would be wise to remove yourselves." It was good advice for as night fell, the crowd became more raucous from drink and anger unleashed. The crowd surged forward, cut the effigy down and brought it to Oliver's house. Here it was decapitated and set on fire. And then anger overcame justice and they proceeded to destroy his house and stable. There was no one to stop the mayhem and destruction because many of the participants were members of the volunteer militia. The crowd then descended on Hutchinson's home and more anger was vented on wanton destruction. Hutchinson ordered the arrest of one of the ringleaders, Ebenezer Mackintosh, a local shoemaker. However, when Sheriff Greenleaf complied, he thought better of it when those he had assigned to patrol the streets at night insisted he let him go. Samuel Adams knew that wanton destruction of property would hurt their cause. They would have to come up with a new approach.

Opposition to the Stamp Act was not limited to Massachusetts. When the Virginia House of Burgesses met to discuss it, many came to listen to the arguments and to the response they should take. Among those gathered was young Thomas Jefferson. He had inherited an estate when his father died and studied for the law at William and Mary College. He was standing with a friend who was accompanied by a visitor from France.

"Thomas, it should be an interesting discussion. Patrick Henry has certainly made a name for himself. He's a lawyer for the little man and now he is the newest member of the House. Did you know him, perhaps in college?"

Jefferson smiled wryly. "Like most, I was fooled by the presence he deliberately projects as a carefree country bumpkin. He never studied law formally, never even went to college. But, having read *Coke Upon Littleton*, he convinced John Randolph and Robert Carter Nicholas at William and Mary to sign his license. Why? Because they said he knew natural law and was a genius. I actually attended his first case. Rev. Maury was suing for damages over the two penny rule."

"What exactly is that?" asked M. Manceron.

"Here in Virginia, Anglican ministers are hired by local vestrymen who also set their salary. Their salary was to be paid in tobacco: 16,000 pounds of tobacco a year. But, when there was a poor crop, the vestrymen compelled them to accept depreciated paper money at two pence per pound. The result was to cut their wages by about 2/3rds. I remember because Rev. Maury was my tutor before I went to William and Mary and he often complained of it, which is why he took on students to tutor. So, since another minister won damages,

Maury brought his case to trial and technically won but damages were not forthcoming."

"Why not?"

"Basically, the British Parliament had never repealed the original act of payment with tobacco. However, the person who would suffer would not be the vestrymen but rather the deputy sheriff, Thomas Johnson, for not collecting the quota of tobacco. He is the one who hired Patrick Henry. As I said, it was Henry's first case. And, his father, it turned out, was the presiding judge. And one of his uncles, Rev. Henry, had tutored him in the classics. Both had fine libraries, which is the key to learning. Don't let his appearance fool you. He is a genius. Henry acknowledged that Maury's lawyer had argued and won the first case dealing with the difference in what he was paid in paper money as opposed to what he would have earned if paid in tobacco. But then Henry went on to say that the king's failure to approve the Two Penny Act was evidence of misrule. At this there were cries of 'treason.' But that only pushed Henry to then attack the clergy, portraying them as self-serving, motivated by greed, and not caring about the wretched state of the poor. He concluded that they were not deserving of any damages whatsoever."

"And the jury was convinced of such?"

"That particular jury was."

"What do you mean?"

"The sheriff, Johnson, had been responsible for procuring the men to serve on the jury thus those who were sworn in were those who would serve his interests, not the interests of the clergy."

"So of course they would be swayed by his words. I see what you mean, he is clever."

"Yes, indeed, but the irony here is he was not only praised by the powerless but now had served the wealthiest, the landowners, who should have paid in tobacco. I believe Maury was awarded 1 penny in damages."

"Well, it will be interesting to see what happens today. Since becoming a member less than two weeks ago, he seems to have already antagonized many of his colleagues. However, the Stamp Tax affects everyone."

When Patrick Henry spoke before the legislators, he enumerated four resolutions that most would agree with; essentially they stated that the colonists had all of the liberties, privileges, franchises, and immunities possessed by the people of Great Britain, thus, only they could decide on matters of taxation. He also pointed out that these rights had been recognized by the kings in the past. The language of the fifth resolve was considered too incendiary. The conservative loyalists bristled at its implication. When Henry concluded with "Tarquin and Caesar had each his Brutus, Charles I his Cromwell and George III…" "Treason!" "may profit of their example." The resolves passed and Henry left Richmond. Some of the members reconvened the next day and found cause to moderate the extreme measures and only formally accepted the first four. But it was too late. The original transcript Henry had written was being carried across the colonies to effect actions and judgments elsewhere. And, inexplicably, there were two extra resolutions that reiterated only the colonies had the right to tax and stated that anyone disagreeing with this should be considered an enemy of the colony!

Chapter 37

Averting Disaster

In Boston, as elsewhere, the Virginians were seen as brave heroes. A seat had fallen vacant in Massachusetts and the election to fill it went to Samuel Adams. He already had a plan and others were in agreement to hold a Stamp Act Congress in New York City to agree on a unified response. The Governor kept writing Parliament that they should allow the colonies to send representatives to Parliament, which Benjamin Franklin had proposed a decade before, but Parliament was still not interested. Neither was Sam Adams because he knew how ineffectual their small number would be. Twenty-seven representatives met in New York. Tension was rising everywhere. Many of those hired to collect the stamp tax resigned. Even Andrew Oliver was forced to do so under the elm tree where his effigy had hung. Now it was referred to as the Liberty Tree. Ships were allowed to leave harbors without the stamp of approval.

Before the Stamp Act had become an issue, Franklin was on his way back to England. He resumed residence with Mrs. Stevenson and rejoined the circle of friends he had made. He had missed the stimulating intellectual milieu of London. When the topic of Parliament issuing the Stamp Act had come up, he and other colonial agents had the opportunity to meet with George Grenville.

"Sir, there will be opposition to such an intrusive tax. We advise instead that you allow the colonists to tax themselves."

"You can guarantee that they will do so?"

They knew that it was not certain that they would to do so. Franklin said, "What about authorization of new Bills of Credit issued to borrowers at 6% interest? The colonists would thus benefit from an increased supply of money in circulation and the crown would benefit from the revenue generated."

Grenville didn't feel that this would be sufficient, thus, the Stamp Act had been passed in Parliament. When the storm broke, Franklin realized even he had greatly miscalculated how Americans would react. This was made clear when a letter arrived from his printing partner, David Hall.

Dear Ben,

You are in deep trouble here. Thomas Penn's man in the Assembly, John Dickinson, has just introduced a bill drawing up a declaration of grievances against the act. They have insinuated that you advised Parliament to take such a step. Your advice to John Hughes whom you recommended as stamp collector has been widely circulated as well as your letter to Charles Thomson. You greatly underestimate the resentment most colonists have of any British interference in their lives. I would advise you not to return in the near future.

David

Ben read the letter and contemplated how this reversal had come about. Throughout his life, he had always been able to criticize and correct his own behavior. Mrs. Stevenson interrupted his train of thought. "You look troubled. Is something the matter?"

"I was wrong. Here, in England, I can see the benefits of America being part of the empire Britain is building. To me, it has always been a mutually beneficial relationship. But that is not how it is seen there."

"They don't appreciate the protection and markets that Britain provides?"

"To some extent but the joint effort made from American militias, supplies, and quartering of troops, seems to them to have been adequate compensation for helping England win the war there. They feel the government has no right to extract more."

"How many continue to feel a connection with the mother country? How many have returned or at least keep up contact? I would think the vast majority are third or fourth generation and all they are familiar with now feels threatened by an outside force. You can see the larger picture and thrive in the culture of enlightenment. However, I suspect most of them have a different perspective. Their identity is more local," said Mrs. Stevenson.

"You're right, most live their lives dealing with their problems, trying to fulfill their personal aspirations. I must figure out a way to make Parliament see the foolishness of their actions. America should not provoke violence against those who are appointed to do the king's bidding; that will get them nowhere. They should boycott. Money lost by the merchants here will have them pressuring MPs to repeal the Act. And, I will contribute with my pen."

And so Franklin wrote to Hall suggesting a boycott and promised to send copies of his articles to be circulated in the colonies. However, before the results of his determination to show the Americans he was on their side, he had another letter from Hall that only made him more determined.

Dear Ben,

Before you read this, rest assured that your wife, Deborah, is fine. A group of your enemies descended upon your new house threatening to raze it to the ground. Deborah refused to leave and fortunately had sent for her brother and cousin Josiah to bring their weapons to help her defend your home. Josiah brought many of his friends and your loyal supporters here joined forces and finally the mob that had descended dispersed. I shall be publishing your denial of any support for the Stamp Act in the Pennsylvania Gazette as well as letters from many London Quakers who have written in your defense.

David

Franklin wrote his wife, *I honor much the spirit and courage you showed. The woman deserves a good house that is determined to defend it.* He then began writing scathing satirical articles using the name Homespun making it quite clear to readers that colonists could provide for themselves and that if they chose not to import by establishing a boycott, the British would be hurt because multitudes of the poor working class of London would be unemployed and starving. Again he urged Parliament to accept colonial representation or lay the foundation for future separation. In February 1766, Franklin was invited to Parliament by the new ministry under Lord Rockingham. Franklin pointed out that the colonies had already done their fair share in supporting British interests in America. His words and demeanor helped convince Parliament to repeal the Act. When news of his staunch defense of American interests reached the colonies, his reputation was not only restored but enhanced. His friend, William Strahan, had sent a copy of his testimony to Hall and it, too, was published in the *Gazette*. Franklin was seen as the best spokesperson for the colonies. Other colonies asked him to be their agent in London.

Parliament repealed the Stamp Act as a result of William Pitt's eloquence, the British merchants fear of the rumors that the Americans would boycott their goods, and Franklin's testimony before Parliament. However, Parliament also passed the Declaratory Act, which said they had the right to make laws for the colonies including the right to tax. Sam Adams kept the Sons of Liberty alive in case Parliament tried again to interfere in what he considered the American prerogative to make the laws themselves.

Chapter 38

Rising Awareness of the Abomination of Slavery

Granville Sharp opened the door to his brother's small surgery on Mincing Lane. While William Sharp had wealthy clients, he also made time to help the local poor. Seeing William's nurse, Granville smiled and asked her if William was free. His brother had heard his voice from the back room where he actually performed the surgery and called out, "Come on back."

A young black man lay on the table and Granville could see fresh bandages on many parts of his body.

"Help me get him to the wagon. He's going to need extensive care so I'm taking him to Barts Hospital."

"My God, what happened to the poor fellow?"

"I think it was his master. After beating him up, he was dumped in the street to fend for himself. We can find out more when he has recuperated."

Four days later, Granville and William visited the young man in the hospital.

"Hey, Jonathan, how are you feeling?"

"Better, Sir, thanks to you. The doctor said I have several broken ribs and must remain here for some time but I have nothing and will never be able to pay for it."

"Don't worry. We'll take care of it. You need to let the bones knit back together," said William.

"Tell me, Jonathan, how did this happen?" asked Granville.

"My master has a temper. He got angry about something and started screaming. His rage seemed to take hold and he kept hitting me, I think with the poker from the fireplace. I fell down and he just kept kicking me. Finally, he yelled, "Get out!" and I crawled into the street."

"What's his name?"

"David Lisle."

"Well, it sounds like you're well rid of him. Take it easy and don't worry. When you're all better, we'll find you a job."

"Thank you, Sir. I don't know why you're helping but I truly appreciate it."

The brothers left the hospital and drove back to the surgery.

"It's absolutely disgusting. Slavery is an abomination! How can the government allow it here in England." The last was said as a statement rather than a question but William agreed with his brother's outburst.

"If I do nothing else with my life, I am going to see to its end. Anyone setting foot on English soil should and will be free."

"I agree. I'm sure all of us in the family will support your efforts. I know your

clerkship doesn't pay all that well, but you have a fine mind, Granville, and, perhaps more importantly, a fine heart."

Concern over the issue of slavery was developing in other households. The Montagues had become involved in the life of a black orphan slave who had been bought by three maiden sisters. John Montagu met Ignatius Sancho when he was very young and was impressed with the lad's mind and subsequently made sure he had access to books. The more Sancho delved into the world of ideas, the more he strained against the concept of slavery. Finally, he asked for and was granted a job with the Montagues. They regarded him as an equal. He was hired as the butler but was treated as a family member. He reveled in music, poetry, and writing. Sancho married and continued to work for the Montagu's daughter. When she had her portrait painted by the renowned artist, Gainsborough, she also commissioned one of Sancho. Ignatius also wrote to those he had met or heard of through the Montague's acquaintances. One such was the writer, Laurence Sterne. When Sterne received Sancho's letter, his reply began with the words 'There is a strange coincidence.' What he referred to was a passage he had just finished in the novel he was working on: *Tristram Shandy*. The two continued to correspond and Sterne published their exchange of letters to encourage others to reevaluate the issue of slavery.

Chapter 39

Will New Ideas Promote Change?

Jeanne Lespinasse's salon was humming with speculation. The usual attendees were eagerly anticipating the attendance of three visitors from Milan. One in particular, Cesare Beccaria and his work, *On Crimes and Punishments*, had caused quite a stir. He was the first to publish a work that applied reason to the criminal justice system and called for its reform.

"Pietro, Alessandro, so good of you to come," said Jeanne. She then turned to Beccaria as Pietro Verri made the introduction. "I am so pleased to have you here. You will find many who were very impressed with your work."

"Monsieur Beccaria, congratulations on a very reasoned presentation," said Diderot. "Your fundamental premise, that laws should be made to defend the social contract, that punishment should serve the public good, is very commendable. Unfortunately, most governments devise laws to suit their own purposes. They do not concern themselves with the public good."

"That is true, but do the current laws achieve any good in prevention of crime. I don't think so. They are arbitrary, excessive, and vindictive. The legal system that is used for vengeance will make matters worse, especially as it is often out of proportion to crimes committed," said Beccaria.

"And you feel the death penalty should be abolished?" asked Frederic Melchior.

"Yes, torture and hanging are unfair and excessive for crimes committed. We need a specific legal code, carried out with impartiality by judges, that focuses on fairness and rehabilitation, not retribution."

"I assume you have read Rousseau's *Social Contract*?" asked Diderot.

"Yes, indeed."

"Rousseau came to feel that the philosophes were as corrupt as the aristocracy in their attempts to curry favor. They mocked the Church but did they make any attempt to create new and better institutions? No, they ignored the masses. He's talking of the common good in his work. The fundamental being the greatest happiness for the greatest number."

"Exactly, that is why the death penalty should be abolished. It is of no use and, as I said, excessive for the crimes committed."

"What is your solution?" asked Grimm.

"Revamp the entire system, educate the people, make punishment prompt and in proportion."

"As far as I know, Empress Elizabeth of Russia abolished the death penalty out of personal conviction that it was wrong. However, her successors ignored such. But, I understand that Empress Catherine has undertaken sweeping legal reform, the Nakaz. Many of Peter's laws were never written down so she sees it as an opportunity to do so and is actually hearing complaints from all and then devising guidelines for the committee responsible headed by Prince Alexander Golitsyn. She tells me she was very influenced by your work and Montesquieu's *L'Esprit des Lois*," said Grimm.

"As was I. Montesquieu's work was seminal in evaluating how laws should be made and carried out."

"T'is a pity that Voltaire now spends all of his time at Ferney. He, too, has gotten involved in legal matters. However, his efforts are aimed at religious persecution. Jean Calas, a Huguenot, was tortured to death on the false accusation of murdering his son for converting to Catholicism. It would seem that separation of church and state is imperative. Needless to say, Voltaire's latest work *Dictionnaire Philosophique* was not well received by the authorities. Nevertheless, ideas remain and spread. Your work will be very influential given the right time and circumstances," said Diderot. Little did he realize the truth of these words would be absorbed in more fertile soil far away in America.

Another topic of conversation was the expulsion of the Jesuit Order from Portugal, then France, and Spain. Most philosophes had mixed feelings, torn between the fact that many had attended Jesuit colleges because of their more rigorous academic training and their belief in reason that had turned them into Deists. The expulsion was the hot topic in the salons. Diderot and Grimm stood to one side at Mme. Deffand's and listened to the conversation as it flowed from one participant to another.

"Did you hear the latest on the Jesuits. Louis XV has now forbidden the order here in France."

"I suspect Mme. Pompadour is responsible for that since they refused to grant her absolution for living in sin as the king's paramour," another snidely commented.

"Possibly but I think there were two other causes, economic and religious. Remember Joseph I's minister in Portugal, Pombal. After the earthquake, they were in dire need of funds. He claimed the Jesuits were, in their lust for power, behind the subsequent assassination attempt on the king. They confiscated property of the Jesuits, not only in Portugal but in Brazil as well which they then sold. And, now it is happening here," speculated another guest.

"What do you mean? They have done a great deal for France."

"Try telling that to the Jansenists. They blame the Jesuits for their banishment and have just been waiting to have their revenge. They have, according to a publisher friend of mine, an incredible underground network of pamphlets that vilify the Jesuits. Much of it is adorned by the stereotypical descriptions they use; the poisoned chalice, the dagger, and mask all representing a Jesuit conspiracy at regicide and duplicity."

"Did they link the assassination attempt on Louis XV to them?"

"But of course. And now Spain sees the same gains to be made, especially in the Jesuits' well-run colonies in Spanish America. They also feel that the Jesuits encouraged the growth of the Creoles. It used to be that Spaniards would go out, manage the plantations and then retire to Spain. Not any more. The Creoles have become permanent fixtures and, as with North American colonies, may not always see eye to eye with the mother country."

"Well, Voltaire was rather scathing of them in *Candide*. However, I did hear that he was appalled by the auto-da-fé of Gabriele Malagrida."

"It seems to me that if d'Alembert is correct, that the Jansenists will fade away now that their nemesis has been removed but I'm not sure that enlightened philosophes have triumphed."

"I may not share their beliefs but it seems that the Jesuits have been used as scapegoats."

"Did no one defend them?"

"It would seem that Empress Catherine welcomed them to Russia as have some of the German princes."

"Well here in France, it will certainly be a blow to our education system since all of the Jesuit colleges are to be closed."

"And, because of their spread worldwide, we will have fewer resources for knowing what is going on in the Far East."

Off to the side, Denis Diderot and Grimm listened to the discussion and then Grimm asked Diderot, "What did you think about d'Alembert's rebuttle to Rousseau's attack on the philosophes?"

"We were all aware of Jean Jacques' mood swings and he seemed to be going to extremes. I certainly agreed with d'Alembert's assessment in his refutation of Rousseau's unfair criticism of us. We want to improve the human condition, not pander to those of birth and fortune. Nobles should show respect for men of letters based on our talent," said Diderot.

"And I agreed with d'Alembert that we should stop providing the aristocracy with a source of entertainment from the dissention Jean had sewn. Jean's inability to cope with his own demons should not be turned into a generalization about society or those of us who seek the truth. Such a person could easily, given the opportunity, turn into a tyrant."

"Well, his mental state certainly seemed to be disintegrating. I just had word that after he got in trouble here and fled to Switzerland, the Swiss also were angry and demanded he leave. Then he was given refuge by David Hume. Now he's turned on Hume and who knows where he will turn up."

Chapter 40

Change is Possible

In the middle of the night, Granville Sharp was awakened by pounding on his door. A black sailor was on his doorstep, panting and gasping for breath.

"Good Heavens! What's the matter?"

"It's Jonathan, Sir, he's in trouble. He said that you and your brother had saved his life. His old master saw him on the street, had him kidnapped, and taken to the docks. Seems he sold him to some planter. Jonathan said you'd help."

"As I will. What's your name?"

"Samuel."

"OK, Samuel, let's go."

Sharp was able to enter Jonathan's plight in litigation and finally the court dismissed the case. The experience led Sharp to delve into the study of the law as he sought to rectify its basic injustice. In 1769, he was the first Englishman to publish a work attacking the disgusting practice of slavery: *A Representation of the Injustice and Dangerous Tendency of Tolerating Slavery*. When James Oglethorpe read his work, the two met to discuss the issue.

"I tried to keep Georgia free of the odious practice but avarice is a stronger emotion than doing what is morally right. Slavery permeates the entire British Empire. Vast fortunes are raised on the trade and labor of slaves. These fortunes enable control of government and its laws to allow it to continue," said Oglethorpe in a disgusted voice.

"I know. I've been involved for several years now and have studied cases brought to the King's Bench. The Chief Justice, Lord Mansfield, has no desire to overturn the practice. He evades the issue," said Sharp.

"Well, there are a growing number who agree that it is an abomination. Benezet, in Pennsylvania, has been very active in the abolitionist movement in the colonies."

"Yes, but as a Quaker, his word carries little weight here. What we have to make clear is the fact that we, unlike the colonies, have no laws on slavery. They are brought here by their masters. Their laws that support this depraved practice should not have standing over English law."

In 1772, James Somersett accompanied his master, Charles Stewart, to England. He saw it as a chance to escape slavery and ran away only to be hunted down and forced on a ship bound for Jamaica where he was to be sold. Fortunately for Somersett, he had been baptized upon his arrival in England and when the couple who had acted as godparents heard of his plight, they brought his case to the King's Bench on a writ of habeas corpus. They also brought in Granville Sharp to help his lawyers. Finally, after many hearings, Mansfield had to acknowledge that there was no English law that established slavery and until Parliament created such a law, there were no grounds for denying Somersett his freedom.

Although it was not his intention, Mansfield's decision was interpreted and publicized as ending slavery in Britain. However, it did not really end it as law is useless if it is not enforced. An Act of Parliament was needed to end it permanently. Nevertheless, a growing number did persevere and thousands of former slaves in Britain became free.

Ignatius Sancho read the decision and smiled. When his health suffered, the Montagues had helped him set up a shop. In 1774, Sancho, as an independent male householder, was qualified to vote in Parliamentary elections. He was the first black Englishman to do so.

Chapter 41

Broadening the Scope of Empire

While Russia had a succession of rulers, the exploration initiated by Peter the Great continued. In 1741, Vitus Bering made his second voyage and came within sight of Alaska's coast. When he returned to report on his findings, fur merchants sent hunters and trappers to take advantage of this new source of supply. Knowing other nations might also take advantage of this abundance, Russia proclaimed the Aleutians and the mainland, as Russian territory.

Not surprisingly, England, with its growing empire, was the nation most interested in voyages of new discovery. During the French and Indian war, as part of the Seven Years War in Europe, James Cook had done commendable work on mapping the Newfoundland coast. Thus, he was chosen by the government and Royal Society to sail to the Pacific Ocean to observe and record the transit of Venus across the sun. The purpose was to test the accuracy of the lunar distance method of calculating longitude as espoused by the Royal Astronomer, Nevil Maskelyne. Cook had sailed the *HMS Endeavor* to his first stop, Tahiti, in the Pacific Ocean, where the Venus Transit was made. He was further ordered to explore the South Pacific for the legendary Terra Australis. Having circled New Zealand, he then traveled to the southeast coast of Australia. He and his diminished crew returned to England in 1771.

The government's desire to definitively determine the Australian continent and the incredible specimens brought back by the botanists who had traveled with Cook, led to his second voyage into the Pacific. Before he left, he was visited by a member of the Admiralty.

"Lt. Cook, obviously, the major task will be to identify the landmass you visited on your last voyage. In addition, we wish you to take a marine chronometer to test its accuracy. We refer to it as K1. The K1 is an exact copy of H4 produced by John Harrison. Perhaps you have heard of it?" asked Larcum Kendell.

"Yes, I have heard that there was such a device. Does it really work?"

"Yes. John Harrison is a clockmaker of extraordinary talent. He was the first to produce a chronometer in response to a contest instituted long ago. His first version was extremely large, about 4 foot square and then he produced H2 and H3, shrinking the size but he was still not satisfied. Finally, he produced H4. We now have all four devices here at the Admiralty. He allowed me to make an exact copy. I think you will be pleased with it."

* * *

England also authorized an expedition through the Consul in Algiers to James Bruce, to record the artifacts of the Barbary Coast and the Levant. In addition, Bruce was determined to find the source of the Nile River. He was quite qualified for such a mission as he had spent some time in Spain at Escorial examining the works from the orient and had mastered both Arabic and Ge'ez, the language spoken in Ethiopia. He left Algiers and explored the Roman ruins in Barbary, Palmyra and Baalbek, arriving in Alexandria in 1768. As he recorded his travels in copious notes, he also made a drawing of all the antiquities he had seen. He then made preparations to actually visit the mountains of Ethiopia to find the source of the Nile River.

The ancient Cushite kingdom of Ethiopia was first penetrated by Arabs from its opposing border on the Red Sea before the emergence of Islam. Thus, they were pagans, then Jews, the Beta Israel, came and settled. Over time, the kingdom of Aksum was an alluring destination because of the trade in ivory, gum, and spices. It also had a more salubrious climate than the hot sands of Arabia.

In the 4th c., according to the writings of Rufinus, a priest of the Byzantine Church, the inhabitants were converted to Christianity. The Jews, or Beta Israel, were pushed further north and then finally conquered. To retain land, they had to convert, otherwise, they became *falashas*, the landless. While most of the Christian Ethiopians wished to remain farmers, Jews often retained their religion and worked as artisans."

Before James Bruce left Ethiopia to return to Europe, he was determined to make one more discovery and thus, he, Bulugani, and Strates climbed high into the mountains where the guide led them to a swamp wherein the Blue Nile originated. The party followed the stream as it grew in size and then merged with the White Nile which, even Bruce had to admit, was the larger of the two. They followed the Nile down to Alexandria amid harrowing adventures. When he wrote up his memoirs, Bruce would insist that he had found the true source of the Nile.

Chapter 42

Winning Access to the Mediterranean

In the Winter Palace, Catherine had summoned her foreign minister, Panin, as well as Grigori and Alexei Orlov. "Gentlemen, now is the time to defeat the Ottoman Empire and gain control of the Black Sea. The long-standing ally of the Ottomans, France, is having financial problems and will not be able to come to their assistance. I am sure that I can get Stanislaw to allow our troops into lands bordering Moldavia. Nikita, please share the results of your efforts to secure a commercial agreement with England," said Catherine.

"We have concluded the treaty and it will provide a market for our iron and timber. In addition, the British have granted us passage through the English Channel and their continued control of the fortress at Gibraltar means access to the Mediterranean. Our fleet will be able to restock there before crossing the sea and eliminating the Ottoman navel forces," said Panin.

"You think the Turks will divert ships from the Black Sea to help defend the Aegean entrance to the Bosporus?" asked Alexei.

"Precisely," said Catherine. "Meanwhile we will move our military forces into Poland. Plus, our fleet will pass between Morea, the southern portion of the Greek peninsula, and the island of Crete where both have assured us that they are very ready to revolt. We will send two of the Greek nationals in the Imperial Army, artillery captains, Grigorios Papadopoulos and Geogios Papazolis, to help foment rebellion and will promise the Greeks our support. In addition, some of our forces will also go down the eastern coast of the Black Sea, over the Caucasian mountains."

"As you know," said Panin, "we requested the British send us experienced naval officers and Samuel Greig has proven himself a valuable resource since arriving in our country. In addition, Admirals John Elphinstone and Charles Knowles will be sailing with our fleet."

"Who will be in overall command?"

"Alexei, of course," said Catherine.

And so the Russian fleet sailed from Kronstadt across the Baltic, down the English Channel to Gibraltar. England had acquired it in the Treaty of Utrecht in 1713 that ended the War of Spanish Succession. It provided incredible strategic value for the British. As the Russian fleet entered the Mediterranean Sea, Alexei felt a surge of excitement. Russia was asserting its rightful place in world affairs.

By the beginning of July, they had entered the Aegean and saw the Ottoman fleet anchored north of Cesma Bay off the coast of Anatolia. It was obvious that the Turks had almost twice as many ships of the line, frigates, and galleys, which gave them far more firepower. Battle commenced. Then the Turks weighed anchor and were able to move into the bay and formed defensive lines. The Russians kept up a barrage of cannon fire, not only on the ships but also on the batteries at the bay entrance. Then one of the Ottoman ships exploded and fire spread to two others.

Night fell. Under covering darkness, Samuel Greig and two of his men steered three fireships straight toward the Ottoman fleet. Each ship was loaded with barrels of gunpowder connected to a fuse. At the last minute, he and his subordinates lit the fuses and jumped overboard, swimming back to the dingy waiting to pick them up.

There were frightful explosions just as the now burning fireships crashed into the clustered Ottoman fleet. It was totally destroyed.

"Great work, Samuel! You will hereby hold the rank of Admiral in the Russian Imperial Navy," said Alexei.

While the navy was victorious on the sea, Russian land forces had moved into Moldavia and then Wallachia causing the Turkish army to retreat south. Soon they were driven to the banks of the Danube but no transport had been arranged to carry them across. Most chose to try to swim across but drowned in the attempt.

Catherine, Gregori Orlov, and Panin had just received news of victory in the Battle of Chesma.

"Alexei did it! He writes that Samuel Greig was extremely courageous and he has elevated him the rank of Admiral. Please send him my official notice immediately. When the Ottomans admit defeat, we can now insist on our ships having free access to the Black Sea. We must also establish our control of the Black Sea's northern shore. I'm sure the Crimea will be an issue so we will make it a protectorate for now," said Catherine.

"I think we should leave the fleet in the Aegean," said Panin. "It would seem that there are several rebellions against Ottoman rule in Acre and Egypt. It is to our advantage to foment these. We control Beirut and if the Emir wishes it back, he can pay us a nice ransom."

"I have had contact with Frederick II and Maria Theresa as well as Joseph through Ambassador Kaunitz," said Catherine. "They are very concerned about our success and we don't want to provoke them unnecessarily. They have martialed their military on the border and Austria has sent a cash subsidy to the Sultan. Therefore, I think it would be wise to accept Frederick's suggestion and divvy up Poland."

"What do you mean?" asked Orlov.

"Frederick has proposed a partition of Poland. He is most anxious to connect Brandenburg with the Kingdom of Prussia and make it one land. Kaunitz is angling for Gallicia on Austria's northern border and we could add lands on the eastern side using the Duna River as our new border. The Poles will be powerless to resist. They are very displeased with Stanislaw's reforms and now the Bar Confederation is leading a rebellion. The king has attempted to mediate but if we three send forces to end this rebellion, clearly the country and its citizens, as well as the king, will be grateful. We can use the opportunity to lay claims to part of the land as a fair compensation for putting an end to Polish anarchy."

Chapter 43

The Divide Widens

In 1767, the new head of the English government was Charles Townshend. He and Benjamin Franklin had conferred on the difference between internal taxation, which the colonists felt only they had the right to levy, as opposed to an external tax on trade. Franklin then left England to visit Paris and Townshend had Parliament approve acts that dealt with the importation of certain items: glass, paper, paint, and tea. The import duty on these items was to be collected by the Royal Governor. When the Townshend Acts were published in America, the reaction was far more negative than anticipated. In Massachusetts, Samuel Adams, his cousin John Adams, and John Hancock met to discuss this most recent usurpation of power.

"It's insidious. If we are not vigilant, we will lose control of our rights. Rights we have held for a very long time. The English look down their noses from the heights of their perceived superiority at all colonists. We are not serfs to be ordered about," said Samuel Adams.

"The administrators they send over are certainly a nuisance. Look at what happened with my ship. Those rogues, the tax collectors, were always paid their money for the Sugar Act duty. I always posted bond after it was loaded. No one objected. But then, that crooked collector took, no, *stole* my ship taking it to Ft. William and claiming I should have paid before it was loaded," said John

Hancock. "All on a mere technicality! And now they are calling for more redcoats to enforce the law."

"And you would never engage in something that was unlawful," said Sam Adams with a knowing grin. The fortune Hancock had inherited from his uncle had been based on the smuggling trade.

"That's different. It pays to deal with the Dutch. I admit I occasionally evade the Sugar tax. But this is changing a law just to suit themselves."

"Well, I would say that applies to all their actions. They benefit; we suffer. Turning to his cousin, John, he asked, "Have you read Dickinson's *Letters of a Pennsylvania Farmer*?"

"Yes," said John, "He expresses our concerns very well. I especially liked the point in Letter III where he said, 'Submission to England's dictates becomes destructive to happiness.' I fully concur."

"Well, he also said liberty should not be sullied by 'turbulence and tumult', but I disagree, I will do anything for the cause. James and I are working on a circular letter, which we will dispatch to the other colonies. We must all coordinate. Their demands will only increase and the troops they station here are an arrogant bunch. There will be more trouble and we must be ready," said Samuel.

"Well, the Royal Governor in Virginia has dissolved their Assembly and they've resolved to stop importation of the goods listed in the Acts. We should do the same. Not only that but we should assert ourselves when the redcoats break our laws, even if only for a technicality," said John.

"Would serve them right!" said Hancock. "Give them a taste of their own medicine."

Over the ensuing months, matters only got worse. Resentment, anger, and venality all simmered, expressed in jeers and taunts between the redcoats and the colonists. Some colonists, such as the publisher, John Mein, aligned with the British and when he made fun of Hancock, portraying him as Samuel Adams' dupe, Mein was set upon by an angry crowd. Before more violence was committed, Mein was rescued by two sentries who stood guard at the Main Guard station. Other incidents followed.

Those colonists who ignored the boycott were also targeted. Vandalism of these merchants' stores occurred. Some were also informers for the Custom House, which handled the collection of the tax. One such was Ebenezer Richardson. When a bunch of boys threw rocks through the windows of his house, he was enraged. From a second story window, he fired down on the youths, fatally wounding an eleven year old, Christopher Snider. Samuel Adams organized an impressive funeral led by hundreds of school children marching in front of the coffin emphasizing the innocence of youth and the barbarity of the act.

As the days and weeks passed, guards in sentry boxes were standing targets of the derision and taunts of those who gathered. When one of them jeered at an officer passing by and shouted, "Hey, Goldfinch, why don't you pay my dad for the haircut he gave you. Miserly bastard." Goldfinch disappeared inside the Main Guard but the sentry on duty, Private White, came to his defense and called the man making the accusation, Garrick, a liar. When Garrick said, "There are no gentlemen in the Regiment", White stepped forward and struck Garrick in the face with the butt of his musket. This only incited the crowd that had gathered. They began to pelt White with snowballs and hard icicles. The crowd now formed a half circle in front of him and he panicked. "Call out the guard!" White shouted.

Captain Thomas Preston heard the call but knew that without a civilian authority authorizing such, he could not call out the Guard. Nor could he leave White defenseless against the crowd that pressed in upon him. The young officer in charge of the Guard was shaking in his boots. Preston ordered him to take out six or seven to protect White and then, realizing young Basset was not competent to handle the situation, led it himself. The crowd impeded their advance toward the sentry box. Henry Knox warned Preston that to fire on the crowd would not disperse it, but only make matters worse. "I know that," snapped Preston. "Why do you think I'm standing in front of them?" Turning to White he said, "Join the relief column." Trying to retreat, the crowd pressed in. Someone in the group jeered, "Go ahead. Fire. You can't kill us all."

It was a standoff that another colonial, Richard Palms tried to avert. "Are your guns loaded?" he asked Preston.

"Yes, but we have no intention of firing. Disburse the crowd."

A buzz arose in the crowd. "James Murray, that blackguard, is coming. He can authorize them to shoot."

"Stop him." Someone cried in the crowd. Snowballs and jagged icicles were thrown at Murray who scurried away. Without civilian authority, Preston was helpless. Again, the voices rose, taunting the redcoats to fire. Tory colonists came to urge Preston to fire on the hooligans. Then, one of the sticks thrown hit one of the guards, Hugh Montgomery, in the head. He staggered and then, in a voice filled with rage, shouted, "Damn you, fire!" as he cocked his musket and fired it into the crowd. Crispus Attucks, an unemployed mulatto seaman, fell to the ground. There was a stunned silence. Preston ran to the side trying to figure out what to do but he failed to tell them not to fire. By the time he was in control of himself, five lay dead. One by one, he rushed to his men, shoving their muskets into the air. "Stop firing! Why the devil did you fire?"

"We heard the order, Sir. We thought it was from you."

Oh my God, thought Preston, *what a catastrophe!*

The crowd was silent as they realized some of their comrades had been wounded or killed. The enormity hit them as they saw blood welling from wounds. Among those who perished or would linger for a short while were two sailors who had been looking for work, Crispus Attucks and James Caldwell, as well as a rope-maker, Samuel Gray and a leatherworker, Patrick Carr along with Samuel Maverick who was only seventeen.

The civil authorities forced their way through the crowd and arrested Preston and the rest of the redcoats. They were charged with murder. James Forrest then asked John Adams to represent Preston. "I believe he is innocent. Young Josiah Quincy will not agree to be counsel unless you agree to take the job."

Adams agreed, knowing that this case would attract the attention of the entire colony and he was a very ambitious man. Meanwhile, Sam Adams, also very ambitious to further the cause of the Sons of Liberty, was making the most out of what he had already dubbed the Boston Massacre. He and John Hancock were attracting crowds to Faneuil Hall to demand the withdrawal of both regiments from Boston. Thomas Hutchinson would finally be forced to do so. They were sent to Castle William, the fortress on one of the islands just off the south coast of Boston. The funerals for those killed made these martyrs out to be heroes against the tyranny of the King. Adams and Quincy decided to try Preston first and they had the support of the Sons of Liberty because Sam Adams wanted to exemplify that, unlike the mother country, the colonies were a model for justice. Preston was found not guilty. Two of the men, Matt Kilroy and Hugh Montgomery were found guilty of manslaughter, claimed benefit of clergy, which was granted. Instead of going to jail, their thumbs were branded and they returned to their regiments. Montgomery would later boast that he had been the one to shout "Fire!"

The new Minister in London, Lord North, revoked the Townshend Acts with the exception of tea. The primary reason for its retention was to help the East India Company, which was facing bankruptcy. However, it did little to appease the anger of the American colonists. Samuel Adams was determined to keep that anger alive and resolved to start a Committee of Correspondence as he knew a unified plan of action that included all of the colonies was essential.

Chapter 44

Forcing Reconsideration of the Issue

"Slavery is an abomination! Remember how Oglethorpe banned it in Georgia? That didn't last long as the other proprietors wanted to make money. Greed would seem to be one of the most powerful of human motivations," said Annibel.

"According to Charles Carroll, one of the leading planters in Maryland, he spends about 12 pounds a year on a slave and makes a profit of 280 pounds!" said Eric.

"That's disgusting!"

"It is and we contribute by continuing to allow Englishmen to engage in the slave trade."

"If we banned the slave trade, do you think the colonists would follow our example?" asked Annibel.

"I doubt it. It would force them to devise a more equitable sharing of the proceeds. However, the Jesuits in South America serve as one example of an alternative. With their expulsion, I have had the opportunity to speak with several of them. The Jesuits did not enslave the Guarani Indians who lived in the area. They were extremely efficient managers and their exports found access to outside markets by using the Parana River. The community was organized in several villages around the major center, Candelaria. Everyone had assigned tasks and while part of the area was dense jungle separating it from Brazil, it encompassed rich land for farming so they produced all sorts of products: tea, corn, sugar, hides, cotton. But it wasn't because they were forced to work. They enjoyed festivals as a community and they all had housing, clothing, food, training in trades, and medical services," said Adam.

"It sounds like a far better life than the filthy, miserable masses here in London," said Annibel.

"It somehow sounds familiar," said Eric.

"That may be because it was specifically based on a book written long ago, *Utopia* by Thomas More," said Adam.

"That's it. You say 'specifically'?"

"Yes, a founding priest, Vasco de Quiroga, wanted to create a society of co-operation in labor while leading orderly Christian lives. And it worked."

There was a silence as each pondered the fate of the Guarani Indians now that the Jesuits were gone.

"It will be interesting to see how Mansfield's ruling in the Somerset case is interpreted," said Eric.

"It's tricky. Clearly, we abolished slavery here centuries ago. However, we profit from the slave trade. And we seem to favor the concept of property. Remember Locke's *An Essay Concerning Human Understanding*. He wrote of life, liberty, and property."

"But isn't the more important 'property' consideration an individual's freedom? The right to our own lives?" asked Annibel.

* * *

Unfortunately for slaves in the American colonies, there were laws that made it legal to own slaves. However, some Americans agreed with Granville Sharp and wanted it to be abolished. Foremost in the fight at this time was the Pennsylvanian Anthony Benezet. Benezet was a Quaker who had immigrated to Philadelphia where he taught in a day school. However, at night, he taught the same material to enslaved and free black children. From his experience, he could justly claim that there was no such thing as innate intellectual inferiority. His black students were just as smart as his white students. Like Quakers in England, he was an ardent supporter of abolition. In addition, he had established the first school for girls. Unlike most, he did not feel that those with disabilities should be ignored and devised special programs exemplified by one for a girl who was deaf and could not speak.

When Benezet read an article that had been published anonymously entitled *Conversation on Slavery*, he was able to find the identity of the author and felt compelled to write him.

> *Dear Mr. Franklin,*
>
> *It is my understanding that you are the author of <u>Conversation on Slavery</u>, which appeared in The Public Advertiser. Perhaps, as agent for the colonies, you felt a misguided need to apologize to the rising anti-slavery tide in England. However, that is no justification for some of the sentiments expressed. You write that most are of a plotting disposition, dark, sullen, malicious, revengeful and cruel in the highest degree. For shame! If you were forced to labor for another, received nothing for your service, were whipped with impunity for the merest cause or no cause at all, saw the woman you loved raped by the master, wouldn't you plot revenge? Wouldn't you be sullen and seek escape?*
>
> *Now, I know that you helped establish a school here in Philadelphia for black youths and I am sure that you*

make sure your own slaves are well housed, clothed and fed. But, at the end of the day, they do your bidding and are not free to be free. I can assure you, Sir, it is the institution of enslavement that will create what you describe. In a free society, you would find that the black people have just as much intelligence, compassion, and creativity as any white person. I do hope you will rethink your view of slavery. It is immoral. It is alien to the values you express elsewhere. The slave trade must end and slavery must be abolished!

Sincerely,

Anthony Benezet

Franklin put the letter on the table and removed his spectacles. "He's right."

"About what?" asked Mrs. Stevenson.

"I am a hypocrite." Franklin handed her the letter and as she read it, he reflected on its contents. *Yes, he thought, I wrote it to defend the colonists but it's not what I want. I've always espoused a middle class where the more prosperous give a helping hand to the less fortunate.*

"Benjamin, none of us are perfect. We focus on bettering ourselves, becoming educated and industrious, putting our ideas of what we want to achieve in the forefront of our thoughts. When you grow up in a society that does not question the institution of slavery, it is difficult to see your own faults. But, Mr. Benezet is a Quaker and the ethos that he grew up in is one of simplicity. And, I seem to remember another Quaker. A friend of mine said that a Mr. Pastorius had written a petition decades ago calling for an end to slavery. Although it was not mentioned, Benezet benefitted from hearing of these earlier efforts. Now that it has been brought to your attention, I'm sure your views will change. But, I might add, don't expect it of most Americans, especially those who benefit from it."

"I shall certainly devote more of my attention to the issue," said Franklin.

"Do you, by any chance, know Selina Hastings?" asked Mrs. Stevenson.

"I have never met the Countess of Huntingdon but I have heard of her work with the Methodists."

"Yes, she and George Whitefield were close friends. He was her personal chaplain and after her husband died, she used her wealth to support his work."

"George and I were good friends. We agreed on many concerns, even if we did differ on religion. I shall miss him."

"Well, in reference to our former conversation, the Countess published an elegy for him written by a Phillis Wheatley. Actually, as the title indicates, it was *An Elegiac Poem*." Mrs. Stevenson rose and opened the drawer of the side table and rummaged through the papers it held. "Ah, here it is," she said and handed it to Franklin. He put on his spectacles and read the elegy.

"Quite moving. Has Miss Wheatley written other poetry?"

"I believe she is working on such and I have heard that the Countess has agreed to see to it publication."

"And who is this Miss Wheatley?"

"Actually, that is why I mentioned it. She is an example of the type of black American Benezet is talking about. When she was eight, she was captured by slavers and was sold to the Wheatleys in Boston. They named her after the ship that had brought her to America and gave her their surname. They treated her as a daughter and she learned to read, write, not only English, but Greek and Latin as well. She wrote that poem when she was fourteen and had heard Whitefield give sermons on his visit to Boston."

"Incredible. I shall look forward to reading more of her poetry. Well, I must do penance and write to Benezet."

Chapter 45

Change Marches On

William Petty, the Earl of Shelburne, was sitting on the terrace of his estate with his guests. A warm spring breeze wafted across the well manicured lawns and a stream flowed on the edge of the expanse. Although Shelburne was in his mid-thirties, his guests, David Garrick and André Morellet, were older. Garrick now owned the Theatre Royal in Drury Lane and was acclaimed by all to be the embodiment of Shakespeare's creations. Two years before, he had created the Shakespeare Jubilee in Stratford-upon-Avon. André Morellet, a philosophe, was visiting from Paris and was best known, in England, for his translation of Beccaria's *On Crimes and Punishments*. A footman approached the Earl and announced the arrival of more guests.

"Thank you, Hughes. Please excuse me, gentlemen."

Walking through the hallway, the Earl welcomed the new arrivals. "John, Ben, I'm so pleased that the two of you could make it. Please, follow me to the terrace. Robert, please bring more refreshments for my friends."

Returning to the terrace, Petty said, "Gentlemen, may I introduce John Pringle and our friend, Benjamin Franklin."

"Welcome to you both. David was just telling us about the portrait he has just commissioned by William Hogarth, of all people," said Morellet

"Now André," said Petty laughing, "You are only familiar with his moralistic characterizations. The man is a phenomenal portrait painter. Please don't tell Reynolds I said so but even though Joshua is a close friend and the king's favorite artist, much to Gainsborough's chagrin, I tell you Hogarth is better. Come see for yourself when we return to London."

"I shall indeed," said Morellet. "Ah, Mr. Franklin, you are greatly admired by my countrymen," said Morellet. "Tell me, have you been to Paris?"

"Yes, I had a lovely visit. I was most impressed with the tidiness of your boulevards. Sweeping the streets daily also provides employment. And your drinking water is filtered through cisterns filled with sand, which must help eliminate disease. It is always a pleasure to see such civic improvements. Perhaps others will follow your example. John and I were also invited to Versailles for a grand *couvert* and met the King and Queen."

"Mr. Franklin, I hear your compatriot, Samuel Adams, has adopted a phrase from my friend Isaac Barré. He and I served together under General Wolfe. Sons of Liberty," said Shelburne.

"Yes, an appropriate phrase. Many are beginning to question the fairness of the colonial relationship with the mother country."

"Well, frankly, I can understand the anger. But I suspect that it is counter-productive. I think free trade espoused by Adam Smith makes much more sense. Are you familiar with his economic ideas?"

"Yes, indeed. I met him on my first sojourn here and plan to visit with him and David Hume this fall," said Franklin.

"Do you think the Americans will push for separation?"

"At this point, it is hard to say. I still think an equitable arrangement can be made but those in power here and the officials they appoint in the colonies are often difficult to deal with. In Pennsylvania, they support the Proprietors against the people."

"Well, if you aren't familiar with Paoli, you might be interested in talking with him," said Garrick.

"Good idea, David. I was in charge of the Southern Department and tried to get the government to give him assistance against the French."

"Who is Paoli?" asked Pringle.

"At the moment, Pasquale is an exile. Charming fellow. I met him at a party at Joshua Reynolds with all the regulars of the club at the Turks Head. Sam Johnson, his shadow, Boswell, and, as I remember Edmund Burke was also present. The Corsicans had essentially established themselves as an independent republic from Tuscany. The Italians remained in a few citadels but were powerless to prevent Paoli from writing a constitution, basically a very enlightened one, the first of its kind. Knowing they would never regain control of the island, they sold it to France. Unfortunately for the Corsicans, the French had the means to force them into submission and did so at the Battle of Ponte Novu. Paoli is just biding his time."

Just then, they were joined by Joseph Priestley, Lord Shelburne's general assistant and tutor to his children.

"Ben, nice to see you again," said Priestley.

"And it's good to see you," said Franklin. "I just finished your latest work for the Royal Society on air and the isolation of one of its components, oxygen."

"Thanks to William, I have a laboratory and can indulge my curiosity of the natural world."

When Pringle and Franklin were in their coach, being driven back to their lodging, John asked Ben how he came to know Priestley.

"It was a while ago. He's a very interesting fellow and very eclectic in using all the knowledge he has gained in a useful way. We first met when he was writing a history of electricity. He added his own experimental contribution by expanding conductivity through not only water and metal but coke as well. When he was a minister in Leeds and suffering financial difficulty, Price and I recommended him to Lord Shelburne as a tutor. His views on science and religion are a sort of melding of the two as he accepts revealed religious truths that match one's experience in the natural world. He and Lindsay have established a new Dissenter's church based on this and they refer to it as Unitarian.

* * *

Later that summer, Franklin traveled with two fellow scientists, John Canton and William Watson, into England's burgeoning industrial world. They visited iron and tin factories in Rothernam and then Birmingham for metal casting. While there, Franklin was invited to attend a meeting of the Lunar Society. The Lunar Society had been an informal club organized by Matthew Boulton and Erasmus Darwin before it moved to Birmingham in 1765. Newer members included Josiah Wedgewood and Joseph Priestly.

"Essentially, it is the practical application of scientific discovery that we explore," said Boulton. "Like your experiments with electricity and the development of lightening rods."

"And the name? Lunar society?"

"Ah, that is because many have to travel some distance to our monthly meetings. To make it somewhat safer from robbers who are known to prey upon carriages during the evening, we always meet when there is a full moon."

In Derby, Franklin was most fascinated by a silk mill. Walking through the factory, his friends discussed the problems and progress of the industry.

"The biggest difficulty over the past fifty years has been imbalance: first between weaving and spinning. John Kay's flying shuttle doubled the output of weavers and then, his son invented the drop box. Lewis Paul's roller spinning frame and then Richard Arkwright patented the spinning frame and the twist process," said Canton.

"And then the mode of powering these machines changed from using a donkey or horse to water power in Cromford. Crompton's spinning mule was a combination of the spinning jenny and water frame."

"And now we can produce 100% cotton, silk, etc. These machines will only continue to be perfected and, as you can see, most of the workers here are children."

"The power is moving into steam. Remember Thomas Newcomen invented the picton steam engine used for draining deep mines. It allowed miners to dig deeper into the coal seams. If you go back to Scotland, you should stop and see James Watt. I understand he is working on an improved steam engine."

The last stop the trio made was in Manchester. Here they exposed Franklin to the new form of transportation initiated by the Duke of Bridgewater, a canal system whereby barges were pulled along aqueducts by horses.

"The incredible advantage, of course, is that a horse can only pull a certain amount of weight in a wagon. Here, the buoyancy of the water lifts the weight so loads can be much greater."

When Franklin returned to London, he wrote his friend, Thomas Cushing. With those in England, Franklin was careful to point out that America was a continually expanding market for

English products. However, to Cushing he pointed out the potential of the colonies to begin manufacturing products themselves as England would not be able to keep up with demand as the colonies expanded.

* * *

Franklin's last trip with another colonial agent, Richard Jackson, was to Edinburgh, Scotland. Here, he was warmly welcomed by David Hume.

"Welcome to my new abode. How are you doing my friend?"

"Still managing although I have to admit, having to deal with Hillsborough sorely tries my temper. So many of the ministers, merchants, and proprietors seek their short term benefit as opposed to a long term relationship that would benefit all."

"Well, relax and we shall enjoy each other's company and conversation. I must say, my stay in Paris as Chargé d'Affaires, was most enjoyable. My religious views or lack thereof are shared by many of the philosophes. Fortunately, my *History of England* has sold well and I can spend my final days here finishing up my *Dialogues Concerning Natural Religion* which, my publisher informs me, should not be published until after my decease as my atheistic views have already hindered me to some extent."

"So, have you achieved happiness?"

"Yes, because I have not fallen prey to the imagined happiness of accumulating property and wasteful expenditure on impressing others. Too many fall into the trap of self-interest and never come to realize that intellectual and moral contemplation applied to improving the lives of others is much more satisfying."

"Have you seen Adam Smith recently? Isn't his work almost finished?" asked Franklin.

"Yes, he has finished it and it is quite revolutionary. I think it will end the mercantilist mentality that has dictated government policy for so long. Adam was very influenced by the physiocrats he met when he was in Paris, men such as Francois Quesnay, de Nemours, and Turgot. They were very much in favor of laissez faire or free trade. They felt that wealth didn't come from hoarding gold but rather from the labor of man. By this they meant the labor of the farmer, the producer. For them, agriculture was supreme."

"Didn't Quesnay recommend a modest single tax on land to support government spending?"

"Yes, with no tariff barriers for goods traded. Did you know that Quesnay was very influenced by the Chinese? I just finished a copy of his *Le Despotisme de la Chine,* which was very interesting. While we associate despotism with negative connotations, don't be misled by the title. Technically, the Emperor is a despot in that there are no checks on his power. However, the Emperor he cites, Kang'Xi, felt it was his duty to check himself. When massive flooding occurred and noble mandarins blamed their underlings, Kang'Xi chastised them and accepted full responsibility seeing it as a lack of virtue in himself which he must now correct."

"You're right. It's rare that a ruler accepts responsibility for the disasters he creates, let alone those of nature."

"But to link it to the economics we were discussing, China's social gradation goes from the mandarin landowners to the peasants to artisans to merchants. Those who buy and sell goods, who put no labor into the product, are at the bottom. Most Chinese are peasant farmers and they create the wealth in China."

"Wasn't Kang'Xi the author of the *Sacred Edicts*? I seem to remember thinking when I first heard of them that they were actually quite democratic in that the ruler encouraged each village to take care of itself and gave them guidelines to do so."

"Yes, and he was a man after your own heart in championing frugality," said Hume with a smile. "However, I think that Adam is right. His work will be truly seminal because while he agrees that labor is the basis of wealth, he does not limit himself to agriculture. Here in England we are industrializing and this shift in the economy is only going to increase. Thus, Adam's work will deal with such things as division of labor to increase the productivity of each worker. It will revolutionize the world economy."

Chapter 46

Revolt in Russia

While discontent was trans-mutating into rebellion in the American colonies, the serfs and peasants in Russia were also beginning to express their anger. During the brief reign of Peter III, they had been promised emancipation, which triggered expectations that were never met. Although Catherine had attempted to actually improve the legal system, the landed aristocracy referred to as the *boyars* had no intention of becoming enlightened and without their support she was powerless. While she might correspond with philosophes and some of the women who organized the salons, she knew that Russia was much more backward and brutal than countries in Western Europe.

Far to the east on the Volga River, Emilian Pugachev and Zarubin Chaika sat talking. "There is a great deal of anger among the people here. It's almost like living in a completely different world. In Moscow and St. Petersburg, the noble landowners gather to show off their wealth. Peter I was ruthless in exploiting the people to achieve his ends. Catherine is just as ruthless; conform to my will or perish."

"Use the people for your own ends and you are inevitably going to cause an eruption. There have been many protests but they are easily quenched because there is no organized or coordinated effort."

"And no way to appeal for redress of grievances. Catherine needs the boyars."

"Whatever happened to the Nakaz?"

"An idea of penal reform that died in its infancy. The committee that dealt with it had no intention of giving up their control of the people."

"Do you think Peter III would have actually followed through on emancipation of the serfs?"

"Who knows? He's dead."

Pugachev stared into the distance. "What if he came back from the dead?"

"What do you mean? Have you lost your mind?"

"I'm serious. No one here has ever seen him. They need a leader so why not him? If they believe he will make their lives better, they will be willing to fight for him."

"Well, as Cossacks we know our complaints as do the Tartars, there are some free peasants, the Bashkirs, and the odnodvortsy or Old Believers who fled after Nikon's reforms. You also have workers in the mines and smelting factories who are pushed to the limit. Taxes, military conscription, forced labor, destroying traditions; there are all sorts of reasons why people want change."

"What we need is to get the local leaders, the priests and mullahs, on our side. Once we have their support, the people will follow. Having served in the Russian military, I know it will be essential to have good organization and a reliable network of informants and spies. The priests can write up and distribute ukazes to promise rewards for loyal service."

"And they will be the ones to call on Peter III to return from his noble exile following his honorable abdication by his cruel heartless wife."

"We must get Salawat Yulayev to join us. He's the hero of the Bashkirs. We will promise to honor their traditional ways, free them from oppression, and, most importantly, tell them that Peter is for his people, not the nobles."

Zarubin looked at Pugachev and said, "Peter, come back from your wandering in exile and lead your people."

By September of 1773, preparations had been finalized and Pugachev marched into the villages on the Iaik River. As he and his army approached, bells rang and the local priest welcomed them. During Mass, the priest read out the prepared ukasy and the people cheered. Thousands responded to Pugachev's call. The first major objective was to take Orenburg on the Volga River, which was one of the few outposts on the eastern frontier that was manned with soldiers of the Russian Imperial Army. News of the uprising had arrived in St. Petersburg but was not seen as a serious threat. When Catherine was informed, she had said, "Put a bounty on Pugachev and he will soon be turned on by the fools who follow him. However, just to be sure, send General Kar to ensure it is squelched. Now, I must return to my guest, M. Diderot."

After news of General Kar's defeat at Orenburg spread across the steppes, tens of thousands were flocking to support their Tsar, Peter III. When General Bibikov arrived and forced the Cossacks from Orenburg, they moved north to attack Kazan. General Mikhelson with his cavalry forced 'Peter' to flee south. The bounty on his head had risen dramatically and Mikhelson pursued him to Tsraitsin. Here, there were Cossacks who knew that Pugachev was an imposter and gave him up for the reward on his head. Pugachev was executed in Moscow. Peter III returned to his grave. In St. Petersburg, Catherine met with Nikita Panin.

"We cannot let this happen again. I should have dealt with it sooner. There are rumors of a Princess Tarakanova. Now that the Ottomans have signed the Treaty of Küçük Kaynarca, instruct Alexei to return the fleet to Kronstadt. And, to be safe, have him arrest Tarakanova and bring her to Russia."

"You think she may be a threat?"

"Well, if your informants were correct that she is claiming to be the daughter of Empress Elizabeth and her lover, Razumovsky, we will be well rid of her."

"As you wish."

When Alexei Orlov received the instructions from Panin, he proceeded to Livorno, Tuscany, where Tarakanova, styling herself as 'Princess,' was searching for a new benefactor. Posing as a potential suitor, Alexei seduced her. Having established her trust, he invited her on board his ship, showed her to a cabin, and then informed her that she was under arrest, and left, locking the door behind him. His faithfulness to Catherine earned him the honorific title of Chesmensky and great wealth since Turkey had been forced to pay a huge indemnity after its defeat.

Chapter 47

Traditional Life Continues

As rulers in Europe consolidated their power, civilizations elsewhere were affected to varying degrees because of the desire to claim resources, slaves, or territory. In Africa, indigenous peoples had been wretchedly affected by the slave trade in West Africa and in the Congo River basin. On the east coast of Africa, Arabs had established bases to profit from the ivory, gold, or human trafficking trade. They had established a route to the interior through Nyamwezi territory to Lake Victoria and beyond. To the north, the Kikuyu continued their traditional ways.

Close to Lake Nakuru, Kogi lived in a village of the Kikuyu people. He had just turned seven and now was given the responsibility of guarding the family's three goats. Wearing a loincloth and carrying a wooden staff, he herded the goats to the grazing area and sat upon a protruding rock. Before him lay the lake that was covered by hundreds of pink flamingoes. He saw a hippopotamus wade into the water. The birds ignored the huge creature; there was more than enough water for all to share. As he watched, a herd of zebra came to graze and drink the cool clear water. A furry bunny sat up and then resumed eating. *Ngai is great*, Kogi thought. Was he, too, looking down from the peak of Mt. Kenya or from his heavenly realm? Kogi felt Ngai's blessing on the earth's inhabitants who lived in peace. All were interconnected and content with their creator.

As the sun began to set, Kogi gathered the goats and returned home. His mother was by the small fire in front of their round grass dwelling that melded into the glorious landscape. Putting the goats into a small corral, he went to see what she was making for dinner. Only on special rare occasions was a goat offered up to Ngai. The goats he tended might be given to another to pay a debt or as dowry in a marriage. The Kikuyu were farmers and did not hunt wild animals either as they were part of Ngai's creation. Kogi smiled when he smelled the delicious aroma of baking yams.

Jean Jacques Rousseau had never visited Kenya to see an actual example of a community that organized itself on the common good, where leaders referred to as elders were the decision makers, not because of their age but because they had proven themselves worthy to be chosen. While many such communities existed, others were being decimated by the slave trade or greed for natural resources.

* * *

In the heartland of America, the indigenous people's lives were changing as well. When the Spanish had been driven out of Santa Fe, two related changes had occurred. Some of the Utes who had come to trade with the Pueblo Indians had been captured and forced to work for the Spanish. Now they would return to their mountain homeland. With them went some of the horses they had tended. Not only would horses help them move from winter to summer quarters but they also bred them and developed herds, which they traded to other Ute communities further north along the Rocky Mountains. From there, they would spread to other tribes such as the Sioux. The bulk of the Spanish horses once freed from their corrals enjoyed their freedom and over the years multiplied. These became known as wild mustangs. Other Indian tribes like the Pawnee recognized their value for hunting the major wild creature that roamed the plains, the buffalo. Over the decades the buffalo culture of the Indians emerged and became central to their lives.

In addition, once having claimed the Mississippi Basin for France, subsequent French explorers had traveled up the Arkansas and Platte rivers that originated in the Rocky Mountains and eventually flowed into the Mississippi River. The Spanish retook Santa Fe and the Louisiana Territory had been taken from France and given to Spain but on the prairie, life evolved.

Although Spain now had control of areas west of the Mississippi, they had little interest in the vast plains. However, they were aware of possible trade connections viable from the west coast in what was referred to as Alta California. As a result, they sent soldiers, settlers, and missionaries to this distant region. The first settlement was established in 1769 and named San Diego. A presidio or fort was built and Father Junipero Serra ran the missions. Many of those who had chosen to accompany Serra were of mixed ancestry of Spanish, native or black. Three more presidios would be added in San Francisco, Santa Barbara, and Monterey. These outlying settlements had to be self-sufficient and, thus, the soldiers were encouraged to bring their families and friends to be farmers, and artisans. The stated purpose and justification for seizure of control in this imperial venture was to convert the local inhabitants to the Roman Catholic Church.

Chapter 48

Controversy Continues

As a result of the American boycott, England repealed the Townshend Acts with the exception of the monopoly given to the East India Company on tea. Committees of Correspondence circulated suggestions as to how to deal with the situation. Some were able to keep ships from docking; others simply boycotted the product. In Massachusetts, the most extreme action was taken when colonists, masquerading as Mohawk warriors, boarded the three Company ships and heaved the tea over the railing into the water. When news of the Boston Tea Party arrived in England, Franklin read about the event and was appalled.

"I can't believe it. How could they destroy someone else's property in such a callous way? Boycott yes, but this will only be counterproductive."

Shortly thereafter, Franklin happened to meet a friend of his who was a Member of Parliament. "Ben, I was hoping to run into you. I think you may find these of interest," he said, handing Franklin a packet of letters. The gentleman tipped his hat and walked away. When Ben returned to his lodgings, he put on his spectacles to peruse the cachet of letters. Thomas Hutchinson, Governor of Massachusetts, had written six of them. Essentially, he was supposed to represent the colonists and their grievances, but instead, he was advising Parliament on how to subdue them! Franklin realized that the relationship between the mother country and her colonies might be vastly improved if Hutchinson were removed. Thus, he wrote his friend, Thomas Cushing, and sent Hutchinson's letters to him as well. He hoped the Americans would realize that it was the governor who was making their lives difficult, not Parliament.

> Dear Thomas,
>
> The enclosed letters were given to me by an MP. They amply demonstrate that Hutchinson is provoking the rift between the colonies and Parliament, not trying to find an equitable solution. You might show them to those who will unite their efforts to replace Hutchinson. They should not be published. Hopefully, they will show leaders there that Hutchinson is the problem, not those here, and this will lead to a reconciliation, not further discord.
>
> Ben

Having been in England for several years, Franklin was still convinced that it was in America's best interest to remain part of the British Empire. But, he also realized that England had to deal with the colonies in a more fair and equal way. Thus, he wrote a propaganda piece for the papers entitled *Rules by Which a Great Empire May be Reduced to a Small One*. He followed this up with another, *An Edict by the King of Prussia* that laid out the following: Germans had created the first settlement in England, that Germany had protected England against France and could thus levy a duty on English exports and imports. German jails would be emptied and felons shall be sent to England. The few friends who knew its authorship thought it was a clever way to get the government to rethink their attitude toward the colonies.

One day, at St. Paul's Pub, Franklin sat awaiting his friend, George Lewis Scott, whom he had met at the Royal Society. Scott was a mathematician and the Commissioner of Excise. When Scott arrived, he was accompanied by a young man and fellow excise officer, Thomas Paine.

"Ben, meet my young friend, Thomas Paine. He wrote a petition, *The Case of the Officers of Excise* and came up to London to see if Parliament would raise the excise men's salaries. Being a writer yourself and standing for fair treatment of all, I thought you might enjoy meeting him."

"Yes indeed, I'm pleased to do so," said Franklin as the two sat down.

"I appreciate the opportunity, Sir, to meet you as I have heard much about you from others. George has been very kind and introduced me to his friends and it is very satisfying to explore ideas. It seems to me that too often we lose sight of humanity, and how to improve lives," replied Paine.

"I agree wholeheartedly. By the way George, what is going on with this fellow Wilkes?" asked Franklin.

"As far as I know, he, too, thinks the people should really be represented in the House of Commons, not just the aristocrats. He has been very critical of the king and ended in the Tower. When he was released, he was expelled from Parliament but the people in his district keep voting for him anyway. I believe he is currently spending time in Paris."

"Well, what are we to expect," said Paine, "government keeps dragging its feet on my petition and defers to the king on all matters.

225

Those who are 'entitled' have blinders on and fail to realize how much times have changed."

"Unfortunately, I can't stay," said Scott rising. "But don't let me disturb you, I think you two share a good deal in common."

"Frankly, England should pay more attention to the internal problems, rather than the American colonists," said Paine.

"What do you mean?" asked Franklin.

"As an excise officer, I can tell you the smuggling of trade goods is rampant. Whole villages can be involved."

"What gave rise to it?"

"It's very similar to the issue in America. War. Wars cost money. Those in power seek to benefit themselves, rather than the common folk. It has been unfair since the beginning. In early days the military might of a knight and his support for a king was rewarded with land, essentially the currency of the past. Today, the land remains in the same families and it is the produce of the land that supports trade. As trade increases, the power of those given a monopoly, like the East India Company, benefit. Enclosure further weakened the peasants when they lost the commons and now many can barely subsist."

"But what of the opportunities as industry develops? Won't that benefit the people?" asked Franklin.

"For those who are in the cities, yes, even if the conditions are grueling and the wage indecent. But at least they can survive. The vast majority still live in rural areas working as day laborers."

"So, one of the changes you would like to see is a more equitable sharing of the wealth?"

"Yes, and to cut out the excessive tax in customs dues. Let trade flow. If we were smart, we wouldn't try to stop you Americans by going to war. We'd do much better by maintaining good relations and having you as a trade partner."

"You sound just like my friend Adam Smith. He's writing a work on political economy that essentially comes down to allowing trade to flow freely."

"Smuggling gangs are inevitable but I've seen the fear they provoke and the retribution for anyone who betrays them can be horrendous. The Hawkhurst gang was notorious and punished any who informed on them. But for the people, they also do it because they can make more in one night's work aiding the smugglers than they do for a month's wage as a day laborer."

"I've also heard of wreckers. What exactly does the term mean?"

"Many a ship has gone off course and ended on the rocky shores. The local inhabitants descend and not only to they carry off the cargo but they also dismantle the ship and sell the timber."

"Can't the people in the rural areas find other means to help themselves? Hunting for game, fishing; there seems to be an abundance in the areas I've traveled through."

Paine gave a cynical laugh. "It should but for most it is against the law. Back in 1723, after the South Sea Bubble burst, poaching increased enormously. Poachers would blacken their faces and hunt, fish, or trap game. So Parliament passed the Black Act. Essentially over fifty laws are encompassed in the act from wearing a disguise such as a blackened face to shooting or trapping game. Since most can't pay the fine, many end in hanging."

"But how can they justify such exclusion? What gives them the right to deny the village and peasant farmers from trying to help their families?"

"You haven't heard, they do it as a 'salutary restraint', to protect the poor from their own idleness," was Paine's cynical reply.

Franklin was disturbed. He had little experience with this aspect of English society since most of his friends were urban professionals.

"The game keepers, like us in the excise department, are caught between their masters and the local inhabitants. And there are no laws that protect the locals when the rich lord and his guests go on a hunt and careen through their fields destroying their crops." Paine paused. "Maybe in America, if you do separate and the people become the decision makers, laws will be more fair. You may have to fight for that right but I can assure you, many here in England will be rooting for you to win."

Franklin enjoyed Paine's conversation and when the young man was dismissed from the Excise Department and ran out of funds, Ben suggested he go to America and offered to pay his passage. Franklin also gave him letters of introduction to William Bache and Benjamin Rush. America would benefit from Franklin's generosity.

When Thomas Paine reached America, he quickly became immersed in colonial life. Bache had gotten him a job with a printer and Benjamin Rush introduced him to his liberal minded friends, many of whom shared his humanitarian values. Not too surprisingly, Paine's first written work was on slavery: *African Slaves in America*. His argument was based on the premise of humanity. How could they complain of Britain's attempt to enslave them while they held hundreds of thousands in slavery? Then, as he witnessed the sincerity of Rush and his fellow patriots and agreeing with them that control by a monarch and aristocracy was unjust, he determined to write a pamphlet supporting America's desire to have a simple government based on natural rights for and of the people.

While his protégé was meeting with success in America, Franklin was running into problems with Parliament based on the letters from Hutchinson to Parliament that he had passed on to Thomas Cushing. Although he had told Thomas not to publish them, they were distributed to many and when Parliament learned of such, they were furious and began to search for the man responsible. Tempers flared and when Franklin heard of a duel being fought over the origination, he admitted he had sent them. He had no intention of saying how they had come into his possession as he did not want the MP to get in trouble. He argued that they were public property. Now Franklin's enemies in England coalesced around Alexander Wedderburn, the chief prosecutor who supported the royalist prerogative. Franklin was called before the Privy Council. Dressed in a simple blue Manchester velvet suit, a demeanor reflecting a placid tranquil expression, Franklin stood for hours as Wedderburn let forth his tirade of accusations and demeaning comments. Few in the room were on Franklin's side with the exception of Edmund Burke and Joseph Priestly. Silence was Franklin's weapon as he refused to dignify the proceedings by testifying as a witness. Wedderburn would have his revenge as Franklin was no longer to be Postmaster in the colonies.

Despite the attempt to humiliate him and, thus, the American colonies, Franklin put out a last attempt at healing the differences between England and America: *Hints for a Conversation,* which he published anonymously. And then he received an invitation to play chess with Caroline Howe, sister of Admiral Richard Howe and General William Howe.

"Thank you for coming, Mr. Franklin. I have heard much about you and your work in science and diplomacy," said Caroline.

"Well, thank you, I appreciate your kind regard and look forward to our game," replied Franklin.

They met again to play chess but the ulterior motive was made apparent when Caroline asked him if he minded that she had also invited her brother, Richard.

"He is a close friend of Lord Chatham, a strong supporter of the American cause."

"Tell me, Mr. Franklin, are you the author of *Hints on a Conversation*?" asked Richard Howe.

"Yes, indeed. Lord Chatham and I have met several times to discuss an arrangement which Lord Chatham said he would present to Parliament."

"Let us hope that he succeeds. Our family has no desire for war but, as head of the army and navy, William and I must follow orders."

Franklin would be on a ship sailing back to Philadelphia when Lord Chatham addressed Parliament but failed to have his bill on negotiation passed.

Chapter 49

Reflections on Future Changes

In Paris at Café Procope, Denis Diderot and Baron von Grimm were sharing a bottle of wine and reflecting on various topics. Diderot had finished his epic work, the *Encyclopedie*, and continued to turn out philosophical works and reviews.

"Tell me, my friend, will the new king, Louis XVI, be an enlightened despot?" asked Grimm.

Diderot grimaced and said, "Who knows. From my trip to Russia last year, I learned not to judge from appearance. One would never have known from life in St. Petersburg that a horrendous rebellion was occurring under Pugachev or even his terrible dismemberment in Moscow. Catherine can talk about enlightenment ideals but cannot afford to practice them if she wishes to maintain power. The aristocracy has power everywhere. Only in England is there a small sharing of power and who knows, if revolutionaries in America like Sam Adams get their way, we may finally see real change. But it will be a struggle. For centuries, millenniums, change has never come. Now that we have growing urbanization, access to information, constant examples of entitlement of the rich, who knows, maybe change will come," said Diderot.

"Well, the Seven Years War really set us back in the balance of power but I have heard that the king has appointed a new Minister of War, Saint-Germain, who has substantial experience in Denmark and Prussian military training and plans to implement discipline and promotion based on merit in our military," said Grimm.

"It is certainly a good idea as many of the nobles who are appointed to high office have little or no real experience. It makes sense to appoint those who served in the last war and now have experience and can learn from their mistakes," said Diderot.

"I agree. However, on a brighter note, I attended a dinner given by the Marechal de France, the Duke de Noailles. His brother, the Duc d'Ayen, was there with his daughter Adrienne. Rumor has it that she is to marry the Marquis de Lafayette. That young man is from the provinces and lacks court graces but makes up for it in title and wealth. Actually, he and I had a conversation and although he is only 18 or 19, he had read the classics and imbibed the concepts of virtue and honor. He will have to suppress his idealistic soul if he is to survive at court."

Grimm sipped his wine. "Do you remember the young girl you reviewed for the Correspondence, Élizabeth Vigée Lebrun?"

"Yes, indeed. She is very accomplished at portraits, is she not?"

"Yes, and now the new Queen, Marie Antoinette, might take her on as her personal portrait painter. I can't remember when one so young has risen so rapidly. Actually, I take that back," said Grimm. "Remember the child prodigy I reviewed several years ago in the *Correspondences*, a concert pianist, Wolfgang Amadeus Mozart. He is amazing! That is not hyperbole. He was merely 6 or 7 and played with such virtuosity, concentration, and emotion. I felt stunned, incredulous throughout the performance. How can one so young have such incredible mastery? It's unreal!"

"He is amazing. Possibly the greatest of all time. I finally had the opportunity to hear him and his introduction of the new form, the concerto, is incredibly innovative. Joseph Hayden has certainly been considered the foremost artist of classical music and when I was in Hungary, I heard him at the Esterhazys who are fortunate to have him as a member of their court. Even he thinks Mozart has no equal. Changing the subject, what do you think will happen with Britain's colonies in America?" asked Diderot.

"Frankly, its hard to say. King George III seems determined to make them pay for the war. It gives them an excuse or reason, frankly I don't know which, to revolt. We'll just have to wait and see."

Chapter 50

The Point of No Return

In the thirteen colonies on the eastern coast of America, many of the people saw no reason to remain a part of the British Empire. There was no real benefit for them and often they felt used as one tax followed another to be spent benefitting those in England. In the colonies, the outside threat of oppression had contributed to the growth of nationalism exercised in resistance through boycotts and increasing discussion of values and rights. Over the decade of discontent, a core of leaders had emerged through the Committee of Correspondence, the Stamp Act Congress, and now, with the Coercive Act, they were again meeting in Philadelphia for the First Continental Congress. Several of them met informally to organize the opening session.

"We must get help for Massachusetts since it is the target of these new Coercive Acts and if England gets away with them there, they could extend them to the entire seaboard," said John Adams.

"They have no right to blockade our ports until the tea is paid for. And even worse, they've taken over the government and are now refusing to allow royal officials to be tried in Massachusetts' courts. And more soldiers means finding more quartering for them at our expense," commented John Hancock.

"While the tea party expedition is their excuse for these intolerable acts, it seems they consider us as servants to do their bidding," said Sam Adams.

"I agree, but also, we must be better prepared to defend ourselves. The militias have to become much stronger around Boston because of the constant harassment and we will need an overall commander."

"Well, I just had a letter from Ben. He's working with those in England who might have more sense and be willing to negotiate. However, I doubt he will be successful. It's gone on too long and too many have no attachment to England," said John.

"Now, let's not get carried away. Our best hope is to stir the producers and manufacturers against Parliament through boycott. When their bottom line is hurt, they will see the sense of speaking up and getting Parliament to repeal these taxes," said Hancock.

"Maybe, but I still think we should be on our guard and prepare for the worst," said Samuel Adams grimly.

All of these ideas were discussed and a boycott established. However, many felt that it was not enough and those attending agreed to meet in the spring. When the Virginia delegation returned home, they now called themselves the Virginia Revolutionary Convention, which met in St. John's Church in March of 1775 in Richmond. One of those who felt the state should have a much better militia was Patrick Henry who presented his bill. Thomas Jefferson, George Washington, and the Lee brothers were in agreement. Once again, Henry's oratory skills impressed Jefferson as Henry spoke with passion and vehemence all were held silent by his ending statement. "But as for me, give me liberty . . ." he paused " . . . or give me death."

* * *

In England, the government had decided that the two most provocative ringleaders of American opposition were Sam Adams and John Hancock. As a result, a warrant for their arrest was drawn up and Gen. Gage was told to bring them into custody and destroy any of the ammunition supplies the rebels had compiled. The informants who provided their whereabouts said the two men were in Lexington and the stores of ammunition in Concord. Thus, Gage instructed Colonel Smith to execute the mission in April 1775.

In Boston at the residence of Dr. Joseph Warren, the Americans were listening to their own informant who told them of Smith's mission. Among those gathered were William Dawes and Paul Revere.

"Will, you and Paul will cover the two routes the Brits might take and we will warn our brothers in Lexington."

As Col. Smith marched his uniformed soldiers in formation down the road into Lexington, all was still. Colonists or Minute Men as they called themselves stood on the village green. Revere had arrived in time to notify Adams and Hancock who had immediately departed. Emotions ran high and a shot rang out. The chaos that followed left eight Minute Men dead. Col. Smith pushed on to Concord after sending a courier back to Gen. Gates asking for additional troops. Since the ammunition had been moved, Col. Smith ordered a retreat and from their natural defenses behind stonewalls and trees, the colonists vented their anger and had their revenge for those killed. This was war.

The Continental Congress was again in session and heard this news as it filtered down from Massachusetts. Clearly, they had to develop a real militia and appoint a Commander-in-Chief of a Continental Army. They chose George Washington. However, before he could organize and equip his men to march to Cambridge, news came of another attack said to be that on Bunker Hill. In reality, it was on Breed's Hill that Gen. Howe, who had replaced Gen. Gage, now engaged in battle. Although he was ultimately successful, it was a costly victory. When General Washington and his men arrived, they set up defenses on Dorchester Heights. These defenses included cannons taken from a siege of Fort Ticonderoga by Ethan Allan and Benedict Arnold. The cannons were then transported to Dorchester Heights. This gave the Americans the distinct advantage, so Howe decided to leave Boston. In Philadelphia, to assuage moderates, the Continental Congress sent an Olive Branch Petition to London as a last futile attempt to avert a declaration of war.

In January of 1776, Thomas Paine published *Common Sense*. The rapidity with which it spread demonstrated the willingness of most colonists to see separation as the only answer. The Second Continental Congress then chose a committee of five to write a Declaration of Independence. Franklin had returned and was on the committee with John Adams, Robert Livingston, Roger Sherman, and Thomas Jefferson. It was decided that Jefferson would draw up a draft for the Committee.

Jefferson walked back to his rented room on Market Street in deep contemplation of his new assignment. To write the Declaration of Independence! Intellectually, he was the best prepared having a vast library of the works of the philosophes: Montesquieu, Rousseau, Beccaria, Locke. *But, the document would have to represent all of the people within the diverse culture of America* he thought. Sitting at his desk, he took up his quill, dipped it in the inkwell, and began to write. And then he paused. *What had Locke written: life, liberty, and property. No. That was wrong. Property gave power, which could be used to infringe upon liberty. Every man should be able to find fulfillment that gives meaning to his existence.* He resumed writing 'life, liberty, and the pursuit of happiness.' Again he paused, as his philosophical intellect wrestled with the hypocrisy of slavery. *This should apply to all* he thought. *But southern states will never agree. It's only been a few years since England began to address the issue; it would be impossible in America. But how to raise awareness? I know I'm a hypocrite because I want to end the trade and repatriate slaves but I continue to own slaves. Yes, Virginia doesn't allow for emancipation except under special circumstances but that's not the point. Didn't Franklin mention something to me about his changing views? I'll lay it on the king and maybe we'll all be more willing to reconsider the issue.* Within two weeks, he completed the momentous declaration.

With some modifications, the committee approved Jefferson's work and presented it to the Second Continental Congress. On July 4th, 1776, John Hancock was the first to sign the document. America would choose its own destiny and defend its belief in life, liberty, and the pursuit of happiness.

About the Author

Daisy Drews graduated from Columbia University with a B.A., M.A., and M.Phil. in history. Having taught history and political science at both the high school and college level, she has written three history books in a novel way to be enjoyable to read, to integrate social/artistic/political/economic/intellectual change, and be historically accurate: *Carpe Diem*, *Is Paris Worth a Mass?*, and *Chaos to Order*. She has also written a political pamphlet called *Uncommon Sense*. She may be contacted at daisyddrews@gmail.com.